Afrocentri

2

AFROCENTRIC SPIRITUALITY

Par

Kiatezua Lubanzadio Luyaluka, (Ph.D. Hon.)

INSTITUT DES SCIENCES ANIMIQUES

KINSHASA

"Mahunga ma ntu an'kayi, meso mona Makutu wa, Nanga Ngangu zakukôndua."

Kimpasi Proverb)

"All those who see and hear the horns of the gazelle do not always discern the message."

1. INTRODUCTION

Africa is known as the cradle of humanity, but how many recognize that the old continent is also the cradle of monotheism? The colonial epic brought a distortion of history that denies to the African the primacy in any profession of a monotheistic faith. Efforts are rather produced to cloister him in the shackles of animism, thus denying him any contribution to the emergence of the great monotheistic religions: Judaism, Christianity and Islam.

In my previous book, titled *La Religion Kongo,* I demonstrated the existence of a monotheistic Bantu systematic theology. The only theology in the world that is fully consistent with logic in all its doctrines, because revelation and reason coincide in the conceptions of the high Black African religion.

This book, a collection of my lectures and articles on the Negro-African spirituality published to date, aims to show the readers the practical scope of the religion of our ancestors, because, for the African, the practice of religion is primarily a pragmatic search for salutary intervention of illuminated ancestors in everyday life.

The notion of divinity in Afrocentric spirituality is hierarchical. God, the Most High, acts through a series of celestial beings that are not divinities equal to Him, but His manifestations. It is therefore improperly that critics have tried to see in this religion the worship of ancestors. In fact, the African in his high spirituality does not invoke the ancestors, but pray to the Most High God through the intercession of these celestial beings, as indeed did Jesus and his disciples!

Besides the practical scope of the Afrocentric spirituality, this book also allows readers to understand the convergence between true Christian faith professed by the disciples of Jesus and the religion of our ancestors, since both proceed from the same cradle that is the Osirian religion.

I hope that this book will help my African brothers and sisters to perceive the opportunity to resolve through prayer the two major problems which undermine our progress in the path of spirituality and social progress: witchcraft and our separation from our saint-ancestors; thus, can we contribute in a practical way to the revival of the high Afrocentric spirituality.

2. MY VISION AFROCENTRICITY

Afrocentricity can be defined in several ways. In general, it is intended to allow the Black-man to lift his head and gain the respect of other races. Its appearance can be traced back to the efforts of African Americans as W. E. B. du Bois or even Martin Robinson Delany who in the 19th century ushered in a vision of the past which included a Black-African "history-graphical tradition integrating Egypt within its epistemological concerns."[1]

Since its inception, Afrocentricity therefore relied primarily on a review of the past to assert the great contributions of the Black-man to the progress of humanity, because, so far, scientists tended to attribute these contributions to other races. Mabika writes in his book *la Mystification fondamentale*: "the mystifying ideology that supports since two millennia the thesis of zero contribution of the Black-man has maintained a true ethnocide in the heart of the entire Black continent, Africa."[2] Afrocentricity seeks to put an end to this false claim of "zero contribution".

It occurred to me during my thesis research that the original African thought is primarily a thought centered on the divine. John Mbiti agrees with this because he wrote: "It is well known that Africans are religious beings; each nation has its

---

[1]   « Afrocentrisme »,   in   *Wikipédia*, http://fr.wikipedia.org/wiki/Afrocentrisme.

[2] Mabika Nkata, J., *la Mystification fondamentale*, Lubumbashi: Presse Universitaire, 2002, p. 167.

own system that consists of a set of beliefs and practices. Religion penetrates so much all the areas of life that it is not easy or even sometimes possible to isolate it. That is why a study of these religious systems is ultimately a study of men themselves in the complexity of their existence both traditional and modern."[3]

Theology should therefore play a major role in raising the dignity of African and in a greater participation and a greater effectiveness of his contribution to the progress of humanity.

My Afrocentricity is not radical; it does not reject the White race and its spiritual culture (Christianity), although it rejects scholastic Christianity and materialistic rationalism. For, starting from a rereading of the data of Kongo religious culture, I demonstrate a convergence of theological doctrines between the Bantu monotheism (which is of Egyptian origin) and Christianity, demonstrating a common origin for these two religions which would be no other than Egyptian.[4] Cheikh Anta Diop joins my position when he writes: "Today, of all the peoples of the earth, Black-African alone can demonstrate comprehensively the identity of essence of his culture with that of ancient Egypt, at such a point that the two cultures can serve as reciprocal reference systems."[5]

---

[3] Mbiti, J., *Religion et philosophie africaines*, Yaoundé: CLE, 1972, p. 9

[4] See: Kiatezua L. Luyaluka, *la Religion Kongo*, Parsis, Harmattan.

[5] Diop C. A., *Antériorité des civilisations nègres*, Abidjan: Présence Africaine, 1972.

10

Two modes of thought are used by humanity to reach the understanding and mastery of nature:

- The lunar thought: a thought centered on materialism and where supremacy is given to reason over intuition.

- The solar thought: a thought centered on the divine, a thought in which reality is perceived as being outside the physical realm.

If the lunar thought is the preserve of the Western-man, the Black-man always evolved in the context of the solar thought; but since he lives in the spiritual and cultural domination of the West and the East, the Black-man moves outside of his natural spiritual and epistemological framework. The entire western culture is based on a Hegelian vision of reason as an internal contradiction within the cerebral cortex. While pre-colonial African defined reason as an external contradiction in which the revelations from God through the enlightened-ancestors correct the errors inherent to mortal mind. This vision of the old African can be read in his answer to any difficult question: "Let's sleep and let the head have a dream."

My Afrocentricity is first of all pragmatic; it seeks to solve now the essential spiritual and epistemological problems that undermine the dignity and status of the African and to prepare African thought for the advent of solar thinking. Thus, pragmatic Afrocentricity seeks to:

- Equip Africans to solve the problem of:

o The fight against witchcraft: Speaking about the blockages that hinder the spiritual development of the Black-man, Oles a Mba says: "One of the obstacles is precisely the belief in witchcraft."[6]

o Restoring the link between Africans and their ancestors, a vital link to their epistemological approach.

o Defining an epistemology indigenous to the Black-man.

o Demonstrate the monotheistic nature of the Bantu religion by establishing the Kongo systematic theology, thus rejecting the assertion that the Bantu, and therefore the African, is essentially animistic.

o Demonstrate the limits of lunar thought and by a prospective study establish the imminent advent of solar thought (the original thought of the Black-man).

My Afrocentricity is an Afrocentricity of the present which aims to equip the Black-man to enable him to face the future in an approach of his own. This is an Afrocentricity that aims to help Africans to address science, politics, religion and philosophy in a solar approach; that is to say, in an approach

---

[6] Oles a Mbâ, *Qui m'en veut,* Kinshasa, 2003, p.5.

of external contradiction and not in an approach of internal contradiction, as is unfortunately the case now.

Among the tools pragmatic Afrocentricity already offers the Black-man in his migration toward a future of solar approach are:

- The *animicism* as an epistemological and metaphysical approach conform to the Black African worldview. The *animicism*, placing God above everything, says that reality is metaphysical and that reason is a series of direct and/or indirect revelations thanks to which man arrives at the solution. So this philosophy establishes the external contradiction as the starting point of purely African conceptions.

- The *kemetic* cosmological argument as a means of confirmation of the hierarchical monotheistic theology of the Black-man through natural theology. The *kemetic* cosmological argument therefore not merely establishes the existence of God, but supports the entire Kongo theology by logic alone.

- The *kemetic* big bang cosmology as a means to prove the convergence between science and religion, a convergence which is the very brand of solar thinking.

The pragmatic Afrocentricity has a long tradition in the Kongo nation; a tradition that begins with Kimpa Vita (Ndona Beatrice), through Paul Panda Farnana and finds a greater echo with the prophet Simon Kimbangu. All these illustrious figures of the Kongo nation worked to solve the problem of the Black-man in a pragmatic context.

The pragmatic Afrocentricity does not turn the back to the efforts of our predecessors: Cheikh Anta Diop, Molefi K. Asante, Théophile Obenga, etc. It confirms their theories by starting from a rereading of the facts of the original spirituality of the Bantu and their vision of the universe, because this rereading shows a convergence between the Bantu and the Osirian theology.

3. CHRISTIANITY AND AFROCENTRIC SPIRITUALITY

Since the 15th century, the West strives to penetrate the African soul with Christian faith; but in this enterprise, one of the obstacles faced by Christianity is the difficulty to make the connection between its teachings and the spirituality indigenous to Africans. Since the genesis of its evangelization task, the Church has rather tried to present Africa as not having a valid divine spirituality, emphasizing that African values have nothing to do with divine spirituality and that they are even satanic. However, deep within themselves, Africans have never agreed with this. This attitude partly explains the failure of Christianity on the Black continent.

It is therefore an urgent need to establish the connection between Christian teachings and the spirituality taught and lived by our ancestors, between the knowledge of divine grace that Africans had through and intuitive grasp and the Christian doctrines. Divine Science is the application of the laws of God for the salvation of mankind. This science was already at work in Africa, healing the sick, raising the dead, doing wonders.[7]

If spirituality, the power to attain salvation, developed by a person or by a system can be seen as content, religion can then be understood as containing the framework in which spirituality is protected, encouraged and developed. African

---

[7] The Black-Egyptian high priest Thoth summarized divine science in five laws and this statement is the most ancient known of the divine laws in history.

spirituality may well be taught in the containing frame of the Christian religion, because the two currents stem from the same truth: the truth of the Word, the divine presence in and around man.[8]

It is therefore imperative for anyone who wants to root Christianity in the soul of the African to understand the depths of African thought. In the meeting of the West and Africa in the Christian context, it is also important to understand that Africans and Westerners do not use the same way of thinking. The African uses much more the intuitive mode of thinking I call *animic* thinking. In this thinking, man feels naturally connected to the divine.

When asked a difficult question a Westerner answers: "I will inquire about the subject". He then asks questions and searches in his bookish knowledge. He is often persuaded that the answer must come from the intellect or through intellectual inquiry. Ask the same question to an old African and he will say, "Let me sleep and let the head have a dream." He thinks that the answer comes from the higher planes, from God through the illuminated-ancestors. The Black-man is more inclined to intuition than to the rationalist reason, this doesn't mean that he is without reason, but intuition comes before reason. In the West, on the contrary, the rationalist reason often comes before intuition; intuition must be confirmed by reason. For Africans, intuition does not need to be confirmed by reason, because they think that intuition

---

[8] See in my article titled: Christ in the Bantu spiritual tradition and in Christian Science.

comes from heaven, and should therefore be listened and obeyed. So whenever the Western rationalist uses the rationalist means in his encounter with Christianity, the African should be encouraged to approach the Christian doctrines by the way of the soul: revelation, intuition, the pathos, the enthusiasm ...

In Africa, there have always been three kinds of teachings: the divine, the human and the demonic. To speak in an African language, I would say that there have always existed in Africa three kinds of mysteries (set of teachings leading to enlightenment): the divine mystery, the human mystery and the demonic mystery. The first two mysteries had formal education settings in the Black African spiritual tradition, while the third was a deviation condemned by society.

In the divine mystery, the power (spirituality) is the result of enlightenment gained through the purification of thought, unceasing prayers and effective fight against witchcraft, while in the human mystery power is acquired by human means. The divine mystery can only be used the good purpose, while the power acquired by the human mystery can be used for good or evil. And as I said above, the demonic mystery is only a corruption of the human mystery, a deviation involving a perversion where power derives from a depravity of thought or evil spirits; this power cannot be used only to do evil.

These three mysteries exist in Africa for centuries, even millennia. The most powerful of them is the divine mystery. The majority of Africans have always been in the human mystery. But the divine mystery controlled, by its supremacy, the human ones and forced those involved in it to use their power only for good; this is what explains the progress that Africa exhibited before the arrival of Westerners.

Thus, as African spirituality was not understood by the missionaries (or as having understood they did everything to demonize it), it was taught the African that everything he has learned from his ancestors is wrong. This poor approach destroyed the hold that the African divine mystery (guarantee of progress) had over the majority involved in the human mystery, that majority is now under the direct influence of the demonic mystery. This has led to a widespread misuse of mental power, hence the fall of Africa.

Jesus taught the "mystery of the kingdom of heaven" (Matthew 13: 11). According to the *Larousse* French dictionary, the mystery is "a set of secret doctrines and initiatory rites whose revelation would bring salvation."[9] And referring to the illumination by Christian way, the Christian Master said: "Blessed are the pure in heart for they shall see God." (Matthew 5: 8). The high spirituality taught by Christianity is therefore no other than the divine mystery. And in order for Christianity to really help Africans, it must play the role which belonged to the traditional divine mystery in the Black-continent: control the human mystery and force, through prayer, those engaged in it not use their potential only in good purposes. This implies that Christianity must be able to develop effective approaches to fight against witchcraft.

---

[9] *Petit Larousse Illustré*, Paris, 1983.

When I speak of witchcraft, I mean the use of knowledge and power in order to harm; misuse of mental power. Witchcraft is neither knowledge nor power, but misuse of knowledge and power. This understanding is important; because it is wrongly taught to Africans to put the label of witchcraft on all kinds of knowledge and powers, thus undermining spiritual values bequeathed to them by their ancestors. To describe, for example, clairvoyance (the ability of read thought, or to read the future) as witchcraft is not an accurate presentation of things. Otherwise, all the prophets of the Bible are witches! Being able to heal the sick by traditional methods is not witchcraft, even though those who heal according to African tradition are mistakenly called witchdoctors. Witchcraft is only the use of knowledge and power in order to harm: to destroy, steal, or kill.

Witchcraft is a mental practice; it is always a mental suggestion, although the suggestion may not always be done by evil thought, but also by words or actions. African witchcraft is also the voluntary use of nocturnal dreams to act against others.

When I talk about the voluntary use of nocturnal dreams, I mean that some people use lucid dreams to do good or evil. And one who practices witchcraft "schedules" his night dream to harm others. And during sleep, the perpetrator does in his dream his evil deeds against his victims. These ones, being asleep, are unconscious of the harm done to them on the dream plane, but they are affected at their wakening by an unconscious mental suggestion. Whatever its form, the evil that is done during these dreams can harm victims if they do not protect themselves.

I do not mean by all this that witchcraft is the prerogative of all Africans, but a large majority is afraid of it. Because of this collective fear, witchcraft in Africa has gained a lot of power, a grater grip on society than in the West. To get rid of the influence of witchcraft and the fear of this practice is what drives much Africans to try to protect themselves by all means, including religion and the occult sciences.

Four things are important to protect oneself against this evil art and destroy the practice of witchcraft through Divine Science:

First of all, we need to know that the power of witchcraft is both extrinsic and intrinsic. At the extrinsic level, witchcraft derives its power from fear, ignorance and hatred that drive the victim. While on the extrinsic level, the witch believed to be driven by spirits or he believes to act as a spirit; the belief in witchcraft is therefore the so-called extrinsic force of witchcraft. Thus to fight against witchcraft is first is first of all to ban in oneself fear, ignorance and hatred; it is then to fight the belief in evil spirits. This is achieved by knowing that God is the only true Spirit who governs us and governs all men, including the alleged witch. The conviction of this truth deprives witchcraft of its power and gives us dominion over this belief, because in reality the intrinsic force of witchcraft depends on our acceptance of the alleged reality of the existence of evil spirits.

Secondly, we need to know that God is the only true Mind, the only true source of thoughts. He alone truly thinks in man, hence man cannot actually receive evil suggestions from anyone, not even send them.

The third point consist, in the African language, to "curse" witchcraft, i.e., to systematically denounce witchcraft, to assert its nothingness, because in reality witchcraft has neither power, nor reality, nor intelligence, nor presence. It should be clear here the process is not cursing the witch, because, in reality, the alleged witch is also a child of God, but who doesn't know it. To curse witchcraft is to assert the emptiness of this evil practice.

The fourth point is of utmost importance, that's what I call the "warning". This is not a formal verbal or physical warning, but the conviction and mental assertion that the alleged witch knows that sin (witchcraft) leads, even now, to death, the conviction that the witch known this as God knows it in each of us. This conviction not only helps us to stand in the way of witchcraft, but it allows us to help the "witch" to escape witchcraft. Because for one who practices witchcraft, to understand that witchcraft leads to death is the strongest constraint that forces him to abandon this evil practice. Of course, we can pray for ourselves to be protected against witchcraft, but to help the person who is embarked in evil practice to turn away from sin, we must understand that sin condemns the sinner to death right now. We must ask God to open the eyes of the alleged witch that he understands that the evil he tries to do against us, he does it to himself violently and it inevitably and immediately rushes him to death unless he gives up. Without a prayer based on this conviction, we cannot fully overcome witchcraft.

It must be kept in mind that the approach is different when it comes to the human mystery. The human mystery implies the alleged powers of the human mind to do good; it also involves blind faith in matter or the use of ancestral spirits on a human level.

Although few people are willing to admit it, the African often can read the thoughts of others. This option is at the heart of African culture. Africans generally know that thought can influence someone for good or evil, and many know how to make use of this mental power and have already experienced it one way or another, sometimes without knowing it. Who is this African who, in his youth, never rolled his middle finger on the index to escape punishment? Yet very few people make a connection between this practice and the subtle inoculation of thoughts which results.

Thus, since the human mystery can be used for good or evil, the attitude of Divine Science vis-à-vis of it must be different compared to witchcraft. The following options must be taken:

- The human mystery is not witchcraft, but its negative use is a practice of witchcraft. Knowing how a substance can poison someone does not make us criminals, as long as we do not use this knowledge in order to harm others.

- Through the prayer of "warning" (see above) we must lead those who are in the human mystery to never use their potential to cause harm. We must pray that God shows them the result of such use: death.

- It is important when introducing the African to divine metaphysical practice to specify at the outset the difference between the divine mystery (the mystery that is taught in divine metaphysics) and the human mystery. When teaching the divine metaphysics (the practice of Divine Science) to Africans regardless of this remark, we end up with an amalgam where human elements are embedded in the practice of Divine Science. Hence many end up using hypnotism in spiritual healing, believing that human practice is part of the Divine Science. At first they may get beautiful results, and conclude that they hold personal power. Personality draws pride and vanity and the fall follows.

- If the attitude of spirituality vis-à-vis witchcraft is the destruction of the latter's, the attitude vis-à-vis the human mystery is the obligation, for those who have this knowledge, to use it only for good purposes. Yet Africans who have the necessary gift must aspire to the divine mystery, guarantee real progress of the Black continent.

African divine mystery (specifically the Bantu divine mystery) is based on the concept of the Word. According to the African tradition, the first human being created by God was both male and female. He was powerful and had dominion over all the earth. The Kongo religion teaches that God had planted a sacred palm tree and forbade this human being made male and female to go round it. One day, driven by the deadly curiosity, he made the contour of the palm and saw himself split into two beings: a man and a woman, two people who had lost their dominance of yester-time. They went round the palm tree in the contrary direction, but to no avail. They decided to marry each other to become male-female again, but never by this human means they could regain their divinity.

One should know that in most Bantu tongues, there is no word for left and right. The expression for Left is the "female hand" and for right it is "the male hand" Applied to humans, this linguistic provision refers to the presence in man of the male and the female natures, i.e., paternal and maternal qualities of God. In other words, the African teaches that the real human being is always male and female[10], i.e., complete in God, and had never lost his divinity. This complete nature of being is the Word, the full manifestation of God in man and around man, which in Christianity is the concept of Christ lived at the highest point, in his time, by Jesus.

To be aware and live this perfect nature of being is the purpose of the initiatory process in the Bantu African spirituality. To do this the African uses a threefold approach:

- Constant purification of thought.

- A life of unceasing prayer.

- Fight against witchcraft as the alleged force that leads man astray.

The Bible teaches us that Moses was learned in all the wisdom of the Egyptians. (Acts 7: 22.). The wisdom of the Egyptians included their religion, their science and their philosophy. Thus Moses knew thoroughly the art of the Black

---

[10]In the Kongo tradition, he is called Mahungu (in other Kongo dialects he is Mampungu, Mawungu, Tafu Maluangu, or Malungila) and the Word is the Kimahungu.

African spirituality and it is this religion that he taught the children of Israel, because nowhere do we read that he had made a clean sweep of all the wisdom of the Pharaohs.

As a learned missionary, G. Carpenter, in his book *Highways for God in Congo*, says: "More than one missionary has remarked that he understood the Old Testament far better after a term in Congo than ever before; for Congo tribal life is closely akin to that of the ancient Hebrews, and much that is far removed from our own [Western] experience is clear and natural to the Congolese."[11] This is normal insofar as Afrocentric spirituality and Christianity originate from the same cradle which is Ancient Egypt. The convergence of these two currents is thus the natural framework that the Africans of today must seek to understand their own spiritual culture and for an effective enculturation of the Christian message.

---

[11] Carpenter, G., .*Highway for God in Congo*, Leopoldville, 1952, p.76

4. THE LAW OF REINCARNATION IS NOT AN AFRICAN DOCTRINE

4.1. Introduction

Since the 1960s, we are seeing a greater awakening of the African thought which translates into an awareness of our glorious past. This awakening, which was initially the work of scientific thinkers, finds today in the Congolese environment a pragmatic echo in the resurgence of theological currents seeking to put back on the saddle the Black African religion.[12]

However, in their efforts to bring the African back to the spiritual values which have been the object of his pride yesterday and which were the basis for his development in the past, most Congolese Afrocentric believers bring us in their theology aspects that have nothing to do with the real Black African religion. One of these aspects, which are either borrowed from the Western occult sciences or directly from Hinduism, is the law of reincarnation. This dogma is falsely presented as a though of the Black-African theology.

The purpose of this article is to show that the law of reincarnation is not a doctrine of the Black African religion. I will use two approaches to achieve this demonstration: the cosmological approach and the metaphysical approach.

---

[12] Among the current which are found in Kinshasa are: Vuvamu (the spiritual movement of Nkusu Nzala Mpanda), Bundu dia Kongo (the spiritual and political movement of Ne Muanda Nsemi), PSV (Puissance Spirituelle de Vie, founded by Décantor, the Church of the Blacks by Atoli…

Thanks to these two approaches, I will show to the readers that reincarnation in Africa is only a belief and not a law of nature as in Hindu culture.

4.2. The doctrine of reincarnation

Florence Wagner Mclain in his book *Past life regression* defines reincarnation as follows: "Reincarnation is the theory that man's soul, or awareness, survives death, and returns at varying intervals to be born into another physical body for the purpose of growing in knowledge, wisdom and self-awareness."[13] This doctrine, which is also called metempsychosis or transmigration of souls, is related to the law of karma, according to which any thought, any word, good or bad acts back on the author with equivalent of happiness or suffering. Referring to the link between reincarnation and the law of karma Robert Brown wrote: "Hindu reincarnation posits a return to a superior or inferior position depending on previous conduct."[14]

4.3. The law of reincarnation is not an African doctrine

As seen above, the doctrine of reincarnation originates from the Hindu culture. This doctrine is not part of the dogmas of Pharaonic Egypt, where most African spiritual beliefs derive their sources.[15] Hemmert and Roudène write to

---

[13] Florence Wagner Mclain, *Past life regression*, (St Paul: Llewelyn, 1994), p. 10.

[14] Brow, R., *Religion: origins and ideas*, www.brow.on.ca/Books/Religion.

this effect: "Not an Egyptian text refers to the transmigration of souls. It is true that the soul becomes Osiris could take any form. But it is not a question of reincarnation itself, that of the Hindus."[16]

It is therefore wrong that most Congolese spiritual Afrocentric movements emphasize this doctrine as part of the spirituality taught and lived by our ancestors. African cosmology and metaphysics allow anyone who leans on this issue, with enough scientific lucidity, to show that the law of reincarnation is not part of the range of doctrines taught and lived by our ancestors.

4.4. The cosmological response

Hindu culture and African culture are not based on the same concept of cosmology. In Hindu culture, a culture that is not theistic but essentially monistic, there is no notion of a Creator God. David Newquist confirmed: "Hinduism denies that we were created by God, but says we are God, or have God within us."[17] In its pantheistic worldview, Hinduism teaches that the good and the evil that we see now are merely an illusion (Maya). To explain this illusory nature Evans Wentz

---

[15] In my book entitled *la Religion Kongo*, Paris: Hamattant, 2010, I demonstrate the Egyptian origin of the high Bantu spirituality.

[16] Danielle Hemmert & Alex Roudène, *Métempsycose, réincarnation et survie*, (Genève: Farmot, 1983), p. 31.

[17] David Newquist, *Natural science and Christian faith* (htt://www.ibri.org/Books, 2008).

wrote: "(...) all possible conditions, states or realm of sangsarique existence: heaven, hell, and worlds are entirely dependent phenomena, in other words are nothing but phenomena.

"(...) All phenomena are transient, illusory, unreal, non-existent, except in the sangsarique mind perceiving them."18

According to Hindu thought the misfortune of man stems from the fact that he wishes to enjoy this illusion rather than to get rid of it. The purpose of man is to get out of this illusion. However, when a man dies and goes to the beyond, he finds himself in a greater illusion that Wentz defined as "similar to the prolonged state of dream state."[19] Thus, since the purpose of man is to exit the illusion, the natural tendency in Hinduism is to return to the plan of the lesser illusion; therefore the belief in reincarnation is a law with respect to this Eastern thought.

In African spiritual culture, things are otherwise. The African believes that the world is a created reality. And in his cosmology, he distinguishes several planes of existence above this level where we abide.[20] The African believes that the good we see here is only a foreshadowing of the greater good that is

---

[18] *Le livre des morts tibétain*, (Paris: Adrien Maisonneuve, 1969), p. 57.

[19] Ibidem p. 57

[20] Kiatezua Lubanzadio Luyaluka, *la Religion Kongo*, (Paris: Harmattan, 2010), p. 102.

in the afterlife, among the ancestors, because they are closer to God than those who live in this plane. The destiny of man is to get out of the illusion of limitation. And when a man dies, he moves towards a greater good, but he still finds before him a much greater good than the one he had reached, so that good on the temporal plane (on earth and in heavens) is always a forerunner of a greater good being on higher planes. Hence, since the purpose of man is to get rid of the illusion of limitation of good, his natural tendency in African doctrine is to move towards infinity; and therefore the law of reincarnation is essentially a counter-nature-trend.

4.5. Metaphysical Reply

There are metaphysically two phenomena that we often tend to confuse: the transmigration of soul and the transmigration of the spirit.

a. Transmigration of Soul

Reincarnation is the transmigration of soul. This transmigration involves the migration of the soul from one body to another; the soul leaves a body for another. The first body ceases to live while the second begins to live. The two bodies cannot therefore be alive at the same time. This phenomenon is different from the transmigration of the spirit.

b. Transmigration of spirit

In the transmigration of the spirit (the power of knowing), the spirit of a person is communicated to another person (or other persons). These ones then manifest the performance of the person transmitting the spirit. In the Bible (Number. 11: 25), it is referred to a transmigration of the spirit of Moses to

31

seventy elders of the nation of Israel and all began to prophesy (to manifest a performance present in Moses).

In this phenomenon, unlike the transmigration of soul, the person whose spirit is communicated and the person (or persons) who receives this spirit continue both to be alive.

c. Difference between the two phenomena

- In the reincarnation one of the bodies ceases to live, while in the transmigration of the spirit all bodies involved continue to live.

- Reincarnation is between two bodies, while in the transmigration of the spirit there may be several receivers.

- The essential result of the transmigration of the spirit is that the qualities are shared with one or more other individuals.

d. Transmigration of the spirit in the African culture

When a baby was born among the Bomitaba[21], the parents were in no hurry of finding a name for him. They inquired with the ancestors to know who "came through this child". The parents and the whole family waited until the child in a dream announced the name of the ancestor who "came"

---

[21] An ethnic group of the north of the Republic of Congo in the region of Likouala.

through his birth. It is this vision of things that is often mistaken for evidence that the law of reincarnation is an African doctrine.

In fact, this Bomitaba culture (found throughout Africa) reflects not a belief in the law of reincarnation but rather a belief in the transmigration of the spirit for the following reasons:

- Unlike in reincarnation, the ancestor who is supposed to come through the birth of the child does not stop living in the beyond, but instead becomes the protector of the newborn.

- This transmigration can occur between an ancestor and several other children of the family. I'm Luyaluka (the name of my grandfather), but I'm not the only Luyaluka in the extended family, as we were three to bear this name simultaneously.

- The qualities developed by the ancestor are assumed to arise in the newborn child; this is consistent with the idea of the transmigration of the spirit.

4.6.   Belief in reincarnation in the African tradition

Reincarnation in African tradition is therefore not a law as I have just shown, but rather a belief. Two conditions lead an African to make this choice not dictated by the natural order of things:

- One can freely choose to return to this plan, because he feels unable to progress into higher levels.

- One can also freely choose to revisit this plan to help his people, who are here to advance their existence.

However, it should be noted that in both cases, it is not a law, but a belief, a trend contrary to the law of progression towards infinity. So since reincarnation is a belief for the African, whoever accepts it becomes a victim, unless he does so by being driven by the desire to come help others progress.

So since reincarnation is not a law in the black African spirituality rather than teach and emphasize it, one should rather teach Africans how to protect themselves for not falling into this belief which is against the natural order of things dictated by our philosophy. The focus in the spiritual teaching should be on soteriologic aspects of the law of progression towards infinity.

G. Conclusion

In Hindu thought, reincarnation is a law in accordance with a conception of the universe where good and evil are seen as an illusion (*Maya*) and where the afterlife is presented as a greater illusion. So compared to this thought, where the ultimate goal of man is to escape the illusion, reincarnation is a natural law dictated by the cosmological order of things.

However, the doctrine of reincarnation has no scientific basis in real Black African thought, because in African cosmology the current good is seen as a forerunner of a greater good, which is among the ancestors; and the natural order of things dictates the African soul evolves towards infinity and not to reincarnate.

What people often call falsely reincarnation in African culture is only a transmigration of spirit. The transmigration of spirit and the transmigration of soul are therefore two distinct phenomena. While reincarnation involves the passage of soul from one body to another, the transmigration of spirit rather involves the contribution of a being higher in the hierarchy in support of one, or several, on a lower plan.

Reincarnation in Africa is a belief and not a law. In accordance with the law of progression towards infinity which is an African doctrine, the man who accepts the belief in reincarnation deprives himself of a momentum towards progress, unless the motivation of the acceptance of this belief is a need to help humanity in its growth.

5. GOD PRAYS IN US

The assertion that "God prays in us" seems a contradiction to many people. For them, it makes us believe that God is in man and this is an obvious aberration, because the infinite can never be contained in the finite. Yet the contradiction that seems to emerge from this statement is the result of a rationalistic conception of things.

Rationalist philosophy considers thought as a personal capacity of mortal man. The consecrated expression in Western thought for those who have a new perception is: "I have an idea." The rationalist thought therefore depicts man as the source of his ideas. Therefore, it is difficult to conceive the thought of God as praying in man, insofar as reflection is a personal activity internal to the cerebral cortex. However, viewed from the perspective of African philosophy, things seem otherwise.

The African, after the acquisition of a new idea, affirms: "An idea came to me." He therefore understands naturally that ideas do not come from the cerebral cortex, but from a source out of him and superior to him, a source whose intelligence is inexhaustible; so for the African, thought comes from God, through the enlightened ancestors. This justifies the old African response to a difficult question: "Let me sleep and let the head have a dream."

As thoughts come in reality from God, it is natural to the African to think that when we pray the ideas come from the divine Mind, the eternal and infinite source of ideas, and thus it is God indeed who prays in us.

The Bible confirms this Afrocentric perception of things when we are taught that: "It is God which worketh in you both to will and to do of his good pleasure." (Philippians 2: 13). God is in His child (each of us) through His imprint in him, the Word, the presence and manifestation of God's activity in and around man. Without the Word man can never be the image and likeness of God. When someone stands in front of a mirror and the image in the mirror moves his leg, we conclude readily that it is the person in front of the mirror who moves the leg in his image through optical reflection. The Word, the Christ, is the power of spiritual reflection through which God acts in and around man. It is through the Word that God prays in man.

To believe that our prayers come from ourselves makes us accept that their power depends on the time we put into them or the willpower we apply to them. Such an attitude invites rather defeat; because prayer is more effective in the ratio we are willing to let God's will be done and not our own will. To understand that it is God who prays in us, gives to our prayers a truly divine authority. Because God's thoughts are omnipotent and nothing can resist them. Since it is God who prays in us, our prayers cannot be without effect, and nothing can spoil them.

To understand that it is God who prays in us also shows us that prayer means especially lending ear to the divine inspirations. Prayer is not about teaching God something He does not know; but in effective prayer, the human mind yields to the divine inspirations. "After praying stay calm and listen, for God always talks to us," I was told by an initiated of Kimpasi (one of the Kongo ancient initiatory schools). To understand that it is God who prays in us calls us to humility, quietness and purity, which are essential conditions for anyone who wants to hear the still small voice of Truth.

I had to pass one day an exam of descriptive geometry that included three questions for three hours. All evolved very well when I finally was stuck at the third question. We were allowed to have our notes during the exam. But I told myself that instead of searching my notes, I would gain time in listening in prayer the inspirations that will enable me to move forward, especially as there were only less than a quarter of an hour left.

Convinced that, since it is God who prays in me, I would save time through prayer instead of poring through my notes. I sincerely turned to prayer. I realized that my understanding comes from God and that divine intelligence could not suffer any limitation. I knew that God knew the answer to this question and therefore I as His reflection, knew too. With this conviction, I stayed calm and a thought then occurred to me that two straight lines that I had in the exercise were parallel, it could not be guessed at the mere sight. Based on this assumption, I finished my exam. Great was my joy to learn that I had gotten the highest scoring that a student never had with this teacher.

To understand that thoughts come to us from the superior divine source which embraces us, gives strength to our prayer and forces us to humility and quietness in prayer, because the "sweet small voice" of the saints is herd by those who are pure and humble of heart.

6. GETTING OFF THE GRIP OF THE PAST

One of the secondary school definitions that I remember is: History is the account of past events. For many people this definition suggests that one should accept with resignation past events, and be content with enjoying their lesson. They agree to be condemned to suffer for a past that, in reality, has nothing to do with man's real existence.

Divine Science does not teach us that we should ignore evil or naively believe that history belongs un-remediably to the past. It shows us that we must grasp the reality of facts: the allness of God, good, and the nothingness of error, past, present and future.

In many parts of the world nations are victims of their material history. They accept the stories as being fixed narratives of events to which prayer is of no help. Slavery, imperialism, colonialism, neocolonialism, etc.., are often perceived as indelible and harmful stigmas. Yet the wisdom of our ancestors inculcates that all good is possible with God.

An error accepted as a fact of our past can continue to influence our present existence. Mortals become the victims of their material knowledge. The only merit for evil to be studied is that its nothingness be revealed, and the allness of God, good, recognized as the only fact of existence. Man, governed by God, is the master of his existence. Man, made in the image of God, possess in reality what he reflects from the All-in-all; as one author puts it so well: "In Science man is the offspring of Spirit. The beautiful, good, and pure constitute his ancestry. "[22]

Everything in history which is not "beautiful, good and pure" is spiritually unreal, and its very existence is that we

---

[22] Mary Baker Eddy, *Science et Santé*, Boston, p.63.

believe it is. Man thus has a duty to put his history in a spiritual context where everything is good, perfect and eternal.

However, to heal history is not to embellish it; but to see it in a spiritually real light. It means to read through the pages of the past the power of the Word, the presence of the activity of the Divine Love. It is not for example to merely highlight the history of slavery with glorious acts of heroism, but through spiritual understanding to banish in us the belief in the legitimacy of slavery whatever its form; to understand that man, the idea of God, never lived, and can never live in servitude; to understand that slavery is only a mortal belief, produced and maintained by mortal mind.

Instead of merely decrying the exploitation and domination which the history of colonization is scattered with, we must understand, as the prophet Isaiah (65: 23) that: "they do not labor in vain." And that to man was given dominion over the earth and not over one's neighbor. The Black African initiatory wisdom, predicting the end of all domination, exhorts us that "there is no stone that shall prevail over its next".

Having their origin in the belief, mortals are often false brothers; they have a past marred with an inherent evil and a "temporal good", both of which are illusory and unreal. Man in the image of God is inseparable from divine Love; he always lives in the present; he knows neither sun rising, nor sunset. Generated in the eternal good, he coexists with Life, Truth and Love.

We can, and we have a duty to free ourselves from the belief in the grip of history and avail ourselves of the glorious freedom of God's children. By the Word, we can rise above a decidedly false sense of our past and stick to the truth. As a firm believer in the liberation of the Black-man from all servitude, the prophet Simon Kimbangu exhorts us: "We must stand firm, because the Spirit of our God Almighty will never abandon us."[23]

7. LECTURES

7.1. Youth and Development: The Role Of Spirituality

One day a microphone was walked around in an American campus, the same question was asked to several students: "What is spirituality for you?" There were as many answers as students who were asked the question. The concept of spirituality can be defined in many ways; it can be understood as the spiritual sense.

A plane flying over our city several kilometers above our heads seem very small to sight. However we use our mind and we say that the plane is great. But we recognize that there are not two aircrafts but one: the great. As for the small plane, it is widely accepted that it never existed. Where it seems to be, it

---

[23] Bandzouzi, A. *le Kimbanguisme*, Paris 2002, p. 91.

is the big plane which exists. So we need to go beyond the limited physical perception in order to seize reality.

Divine metaphysics, as taught and lived by our ancestors, was above all an "eye opening", i.e., the acquisition of spiritual sense; because in his conception of the universe, the Black African man affirms that reality is beyond the phenomenon called by the modern matter; so we need the spiritual sense, or spirituality to perceive reality.

The children of London remember the story of Dick Whittington; he worked in a hotel in this city, and though giving the best of himself, Dick was not loved by people. He was criticized; none liked whatever he was doing, so that one day, discouraged, he decided to leave London. But once at the borders of the city, he heard a bell ringing out; in the sound of the bell, he discerned a voice saying to him: "Dick, return three times Mayor of London." It is thanks to his spirituality, his spiritual sense, that Dick heard that voice.

He quickly realized that God had spoken to him. Convinced that he mattered to God, Dick was also convinced that even men should have respect for him. From that moment, he had a new perspective on himself. He returned to the hotel, and since his vision of himself had changed, his experience also became different, people began to appreciate his work, he became quickly the best worker of the enterprise, and he ended up marrying the boss' daughter. At the death of his father-in-law, Dick became the new owner of the business; he had lots of money. He then launched into the electoral race for the mayoral of London; he was elected Mayor of London once, then a second and a third time as the bell sounded.

Spirituality is natural to all of us. The Bassa of Cameroon call man *mut*, but to distinguish the *mut* from the mortal they see, they call mortal man (whose Paul calls the old man): *mut binam*; i.e., the man who has two hands and two legs. It is thanks to their natural spirituality that the Bassa know that the real man is more than the common person we see.

But though spirituality is natural to all of us, we must develop it. Jesus said in the Gospel of Mathew: "Blessed are the pure in heart for they shall see God."[24] This leads to the understanding that the way to develop the spiritual sense, the sense that allows us to see what is invisible to the corporeal sense, is the purification.

Here is a very simple approach for those who want to work for the purification of their thoughts:

- Affirm one's purity as a child of God: "I am pure, I have always been pure, and I will always be pure;" This implies that one must not see sin as part of his real being.

- If while declaring one's purity past sins remembrance flood in the mind, one must:

    o Recognize the sin that was committed. If one does not recognize that in the decimal base 1 +1 is not equal to 89, one cannot be a good mathematicians. But to recognize that this is a

---

[24] *Matthieu* 5: 8.

45

mistake is a proof of being good in arithmetic; since one can thus correct the mistake. It is the same with sin, the one who recognizes his sin is a good believer, and he can reform himself.

o   Separate the sin from one's true identity as a child of God who has always been pure.

o   Realize and affirm that this sin never did one any good; hence it cannot separate man from God. The alleged strength of sin is the belief that it did one good, or that it can do another one good. To destroy this belief and commit one's life to this conviction brings the real reform.

•   Reaffirm one's purity: "I am pure, I have always been pure, and I will always be pure."

If we apply ourselves to pray in this way, and to align our thoughts and our actions with our prayers, memories of sin will come less and less to thought, until they completely disappear thanks to the reform.

I do not expect that after reading this article everyone will perfectly demonstrates holiness. Nobody expects that at his first steps a child can run. We even know that he can fall; hence we surround him with arms. If each time he falls, the child stands up and tries again; he will eventually walk and even run. No matter if we happen to fall into sin again, we must rise affirming and understanding that sin never did us any good and move forward. The more we will arise and go forward the less we will fall.

Afrocentric divine metaphysics teaches us that man was created male and female and had dominion over all the earth (the Bakongo call this real nature of man Kimahungu). Thus, as we have seen for the Bassa, man is spiritual. To become aware of this reality and live it is the purpose of the high Black African initiation; so this initiation focuses on the development of spirituality.

Spirituality can help us develop our talents, as we have seen in the case of Dick Wittington. The true story of Frank Magwegwe also illustrates this fact. Walking one day by the window of the reading room of a church, a display of books on spirituality drew his attention. He decided to enter and inquire on what he had read about the true nature of man in a book on divine Science that was exposed. Becoming aware of his true identity as described in this book, he decided to put into practice the little talent he thought he had.

He began selling vegetables for someone. However he continued to study the divine Science to increase his knowledge of God, of the Word and of man made in the image of God that each of us represents. As he used his talents and relied on prayer, they began to increase gradually as his understanding of God increased.

Soon, he opened his own display selling vegetables, where he employed someone. Later a gentleman noticed that Frank had a basic instruction that could allow him to go to university. Thanks to a scholarship, he graduated and today he is a great South African businessman.

Spirituality helps us to use our talents in ways of progress and for the good of humanity, as the example of Ray Conniff, a jazz musician shows it. One day, said Ray in an interview with *Christian Science Sentinel*[25], he received a letter from a lady in South America. His parents had died when she was ten years old; she went to live with an aunt who mistreated her. Her fifteenth anniversary was very sad; no party, no gift, everyone had forgotten her. She decided to take a bunch of pills to "sleep forever". Suddenly, she heard music coming from a field. Something in the song changed his attitude. She went to sleep. The next day, she threw the pills and chose to live. The music she heard was the recording of *Bésame mucho* by Ray Connif. She was forty-five years old when she wrote to the jazzman. She was married and had children. There was something for her in this song.

Now you're wondering what brought the cure of this girl. Here is Ray's answer: "During the concerts, before and after - and every time - I pray: 'Father, help me to express good things, help me for the rhythm, help me to interpret the music.' I always pray that way." Here is someone who uses spirituality in his work to bless humanity. Ray knows that music is more than notes, and spiritual vision led him to use prayer in his career.

Mary Baker Eddy wrote in his book *Science and Health*: "progress is the law of God, that law requires us only what we can certainly accomplish."[26] We know that the law in its nature

---

[25] Interview of Ray Conniff, in *the Christian Science Sentinel*, 24 may 1990.

[26] Mary Baker Eddy, *Science et Santé*, Boston: CSPS, 1989, p. 233.

is universal and inevitable; your progress, the progress of your nation is something inevitable. The author adds that progress requires of us only what we can do, nothing more; finally, she shows us that it is a certainty: we can certainly accomplish it. All that seems to say otherwise is a lie.

After World War II many American companies were closed. A New York firm specialized in buying these plants; it used to sell them after reactivation. Everything worked well until the day they bought a paper mill. They sent an engineer after another, but nothing worked; sometimes it was spare parts which could not be found, other times water supply was the trouble; problems arose at any time that hampered the proper functioning of the enterprise; these gentlemen did not succeed because they accept evil as a reality.

But, it happened that whenever the bad news arrived at headquarter an employee of the administration, who was studying divine Science, refused to admit them in the depths of his heart; because he thought: a machine cannot resist the divine intelligence. This gentleman, instead of relying on the material senses like the others, he instead relied on the spiritual sense, in other words on his spirituality.

One day, out of the blue, the head of the enterprise decided to send this gentleman to run this paper mill. This employee was first afraid; as an administrative officer how could he succeed where engineers had failed and the enterprise was indeed in the field of engineering. But remembering his prayers, he understood that God gave him this as an opportunity to prove the veracity of his affirmations about the situation.

So he went to his new job. At the beginning nothing seemed to work, as usual, and he sought the help of a spiritual healer who agreed to pray for him. This one made him understand that he had to get rid of fear.

Fear is not a heart pounding. To fear is to believe that evil is a power. If we refuse to accept that evil has power by realizing that God has all power, we have no fear.

This gentleman put away fear, and things started to flip very well. In less than a month, the firm already turned at one hundred percent of its performance. The man was made a member of the board of the enterprise. Through spirituality, he saved jobs; he participated in the development of humanity and in his own development.[27]

God created each of us in his image and likeness. We can all begin to perceive our true identity if we turn to the spiritual sense, our ability to perceive the divine. The possession of this spiritual sense is our spirituality. We can increase our spirituality through daily purification of our consciousness. With spirituality each of us will be an instrument for the development of his environment.

7.2. The Art of Spiritual Reconstruction

Reconstruction is a constant demand that we face in our lives on various levels: health, education, profession, relations… To rebuild spiritually the present is first of all to

---

[27] *A century of Christian Science healing*, Boston: CSPS, 1966, pp. 189-191.

heal the past. We often tend to believe that the past is something fixed; facts which are not within the reach of any remedy and of which we must resign ourselves to suffer the consequences. But in reality nothing is out of the reach of the healing power of the Word, the constant activity of divine love, even in our past!

Many years ago, I had to go to a travel agent for some information. At the bus stop, the conductor of the first bus that came refused to let me in. Rather than get angry, grieve, or consider that this situation was over and that I could do nothing about it; I affirmed that this refusal could only lead to my good. I was basing my reason on a passage from the Epistle of Paul to the Romans which says: "We know, moreover, that all things work together for good to them that love God, to them who are called according to his purpose." (Romans 8: 28) I was able to board the next bus.

On my getting off, I had to walk a distance to reach the travel bureau. However, the precise moment I reached an intersection, I saw a taxi passing and inside was a friend who had the information that needed, and he could shout it without stopping the taxi. A minute late or a minute in advance, I could not enjoy this happy coincidence. The truth that I asserted after missing my first bus brought the situation to my advantage.

We do not have to take the past as irrecoverable, we can use the spiritual law which Paul refers to correct any past situation.

To heal the past often involves the exercise of forgiveness. However to forgive is not to say of someone: he did me this or that but I forgave. True forgiveness implies the understanding that in reality no one did us evil; because God is omnipresent and omnipotent. The first recipient of forgiveness is the victim; the offender can be benefited only insofar he changes through reform.

To rebuild a demolished house, we start by removing demolition debris. But it is not enough to remove the physical debris we must also remove mental debris caused by a criminal demolition: fear, hatred, discouragement, sadness, etc.; because these errors can hamper the work of reconstruction more than the physical debris.

To rebuild spiritually we must fix our thoughts on God rather than on the debris. The story of a sailor illustrates this fact. He had to unwind a rope attached at the top of a long mat. So he climbed to the top of this endless mat and performed his work. However at the moment he wanted to descend, he looked down, and seeing the long distance that separated him from the hull, he was very scared and grabbed the pole to the point that he could not go down. An experienced sailor saw what was happening gave him a very simple advice: "Fix your eyes on high, and begins to descend." Staring away from the object of his fear, he began to go down quietly, eyes fixed to the sky.

Often in front of the task of reconstruction, we fix our thinking on the colossal nature of the work to be done, or to its complexity, and this scares us, and ultimately discourages us, thus blocking any progress. The history of the sailor shows us that we should rather turn our gaze to God, the Most High, toward the divine Mind, the infinite source of spiritual ideas we need to move forward.

To rebuild spiritually is to heal; it is to see the past in a spiritual way, this gives us a positive perspective of the present and the future. A friend of mine was faced with an experience that illustrates this truth. He stood with his family in a distant city where he was doing trade between two countries. Everything worked fine, until someone asked him to quickly grow the amount of their money by getting into the fuel business. He gave all his capital to this man in the hope of receiving the stock that would make his business prosper. Once in possession of this money, this partner disappeared in the wild. My friend found himself stripped of all his capital and with a family to feed without other forms of support.

However he decided to spiritually rebuild his destroyed trade. He knew that the first step was to heal this past of robbery; so he worked first to forgive this partner, understanding that nothing could separate him from good, because good is God. Then, watching over his thoughts, and turning completely to God, he refused to let in any thought of doubt, fear, or regret. With the money of household he took from her wife, he started a small business with courage. Many happy circumstances presented themselves on his way so that in a short time he even exceeded the amount of the former capital, and later, he found a good job in an oil company.

Nothing can stop the endless stream of good flowing from Divine Love. In my childhood, we lived near a river where we liked to play. The game consisted in stopping little sources that abounded at the edge of the river; it was a simple game, just locate one of those source and flatten it with both hands. For a few moments the flow stops, then you see water spring between your fingers. If with our two hands and all our might we cannot stop a little source, who can stop God, the infinite source which pours infinite good?

To rebuild spiritually the present implies first of all to heal the past. For that we can avail ourselves of the spiritual law that tells us that "all things work together for good to them that love God..." (Romans 8: 28). To heal the past may require of us to forgive. True forgiveness is in the understanding that in reality no one did us any evil; because God is omnipresent and omnipotent good. Forgiveness sets us free to move onward, but the culprit is benefited thereof only as he goes through reformation. To rebuild spiritually we must get rid of mental debris and fix our thoughts on God, the infinite source of all good.

7.3.   Incurability is a Lie

A tourist guide, wanting to give visitors of a grotto an idea of complete darkness, turned off the light right in the middle of the tour. Darkness in the grotto was such that nobody could even see his own fingers. The guide then took a match from his pocket and lit it; with that little glow, the group could again move forward. This experience, lived in the bowels of the earth, teaches us an important lesson: whatever the nature of darkness, it can not withstand the slightest light.

When a child was born into the traditional Bantu society, he was showed the sun. By this primordial gesture the infants learned the first and most important lesson of the Afrocentric spirituality: man is actually a sun, an eternal irradiation of the infinite glory of the Most High God. Since man is a sun then God, the Most High, is more than the sun-of-sun, He is Light.

In God, the light, there is not the slightest darkness. The divine light, or Truth, is omnipresent, it fills every being. God is All-in-all; everything in His universe manifests His nature. Thus, evil is not part of creation, as light and darkness can not dwell together. Light as God, the Most High can not produce darkness; which implies that God is not the source of evil.

The Kongo spiritual tradition refers to the devil as "nkadi ampemba" term which implies: the rejection of the truth, of the law. In the tradition of the Ibgo (Nigeria), the same devil is "ekwensu" which is probably a contraction of the expression "ekwe ensu" (if you accept, it will happen). These African expressions show that in the Afrocentric spirituality, the devil is not a personal being, but an impersonal false suggestion that must be rejected. So evil has only the power we give it in our ignorance.

Man is actually the image and likeness of God. In him dwells the fullness of the Godhead, the Word. To express this perfection of being, the Bantus call the right side of their body male and the left female. As the image of God, man is therefore the expression of the infinite light, so he is a sun, as I pointed out above. Evil is not therefore part of the divine man. Evil is a false suggestion that man should reject whatever its duration.

God is Omnipotent; whatever the nature evil assumes, it has no real power. The daughter of a friend had a case of acute verminosis. The child had excruciating pain and her stature became visibly deformed. The case had resisted all allopathic medical treatments. Following the advice of a mom who invited the family to use spiritual treatment, the child was carried to a spiritual healer.

The healer made it clear to the mother and the child that it is to man that God gave dominion over the worms and not the reverse. The African in his high spirituality understands that the universe reflects the divine nature so that it can not harm humans. Echoing this view of nature the Bible says: "God saw everything he had made, and behold it was very good." (Genesis 1: 31.) The word "all" in this verse includes worms. God does not know parasitism, it is He who takes care of everything in the universe, so that worms and microbes do not actually need to live at the expense of man, and this is of all the more true that to man was given dominion over everything.

With this understanding the child was cured while not a single worm came out of his belly. Pain ceased and the child resumed his normal form. Healing was complete and permanent.

Belief in the incurability is sometimes linked to the fact that disease is seen as a punishment from God due to sin. It is true that Afrocentric spirituality tells us that sin leads to death. Being light, God knows neither sin nor the disease. As we turn our back to God, sin necessarily turns us away from all good, because God is good; hence sin leads to death.

However, man, made in the image of God, is inseparable from the Word, the presence of the divine nature. Whatever be the past, present, or future nature of sin, man can overcome and defeat the evil which results from the transgression. To understand that sin never really did us any good and take the path of reform on this basis provides us victory over the consequences of sin.

A young woman and her baby had a chronic illness that defied any attempt of healing through material medical means. She decided to rely on a treatment through prayer. It became clear during this treatment that their evil was the result of hatred she maintained against her neighbor. The spiritual healer advised her to assert the spiritual nature of his neighbor whenever she thought of her and to understand that nature as the only one she has. Having accepted the power of love in her life, they were both completely healed.

God, the Most High, is omnipotent and omnipresent. He is light, and in Him there is no darkness. Whatever its nature, disease is not from God, and therefore has in reality no power over man in the image and likeness of God that each of us really is. The omnipotence of God, removes to evil any pretense of power; thus incurability is a lie.

7.4.   Hope in Adversity

The existence on this earth is marked with circumstances that can occasionally appear to us as insurmountable hardships. Yet the lives of famous men and women prove that the troubles are only opportunities to go further in our demonstration of the infinite goodness of the Most High. Norman Nel illustrates this fact in his book *English and Afrikaans jokes*.

Nel said that one day a farmer's donkey fell into a deep well. Seeing the situation, the helpless farmer consoled himself by saying that the animal was too old and given the great depth of the well, it was not worth the trouble to get the donkey out of it; after all, it was an opportunity to get rid of a useless well. So he decided to fill the well with the content of his agricultural discharge. He invited his friends to help him accomplish this task.

When the donkey felt on his back the first pile of rubbish and realized what was happening, panicked, it shouted with all its might. But its cries changed nothing in the resolution of the farmers. The donkey then kept quiet and it thought, and the idea came to it to shake itself violently. It then realized that dirt fell down and it could ascend over the fallen dirt. So that after a while the farmers said, "let's see where we stand with the amount we have already poured into the hole." To their astonishment, they found that the donkey was almost at the edge of the well.

This story is a great lesson for us when we are faced with adverse situations. It shows us the necessity in adversity to recall that we need:

- To banish fear.

- To be calm and lend ear to God.

- To Shake evil,

- To get above the belief in error.

Let's examine each of these points:

e. **Banish fear**

In an adversarial position our first enemy is fear. Fear tends to magnify the problem by presupposing that evil is powerful and that good is beyond our reach. Fear is the first feeling that the disciple of the ancient initiatory academies had to overcome before being accepted to receive the secret teachings. We destroy fear by understanding that God's omnipotence excludes the presence of another power called evil. God being power, evil, the opposite of God, good, can not have power. Fear is an alarming condition which tends to cut us off from our spiritual senses and impede us to listen to the voice of God.

f. Being calm and lending ear to God

To banish fear allows us to be quiet. The importance of being calm is justified by the fact that in the Black African epistemology, it is understood that ideas come to man. The ideas come from a source outside man and superior to our humanity: God.

It is difficult to hear the voice of God speaking to us through the illuminated ancestors, if we have the mind riveted to evil. A Bantu wisdom says: "The ear does not hear two at the same time."[28]

Being calm is a divine quality; the voice of God can only be calm and gentle. Heavenly inspirations come to us by a barely audible voice or through intuitions.

g. Shake evil

We must never let the devil quiet because it gives him the false impression of being victorious. We shake evil by knowing

---

[28] « *Kutu kawânga kôle ko.* » Proverbe Kongo.

and affirming that evil has no power, as we said above. But also by knowing and affirming that evil can not prevent us from expressing our identity. Whatever obscure may be the darkness, it can never extinguish the flame of the Word that shines forever in man.

To shake evil is to refuse to give him the assurance of having us in its grip. By our assurance of Truth, of the invulnerability of our divine identity against evil, we bring evil and those that lend themselves to serve it to doubt their hold on us. The spiritual identity is the only one we really have here and now. And this identity forever protected by the Word, is out of reach of evil. The conviction of this truth held in the mind, pushes the evil to fall under the boomerang effect of its own fear.

h. Rise above the belief in the error

To rise above error is to first understand that evil is only a suggestion. Mortal mind is always trying to make us believe that evil is a state of matter, that the disease is a condition of our body, or that evil is a belief that we have in our mind and that we have to make efforts to get rid of.

Divine Science teaches us that evil is not a state of matter or of the body, neither is it a presence of a mistaken belief in our thinking, but rather a false suggestion that comes to our mind that we do not handle at all or do not handle correctly. The evil only claims to be, but it does not have the power to penetrate our identity.

To make an effort to ward off evil of our thinking is precisely to accept that we are a victim of evil. Whatever its nature or its duration evil is no more than a suggestion and we must always work to refuse to accept the erroneous suggestions rather than work to rid ourselves of a belief.

The Bible shows us by the story of Elijah the need to be calm and rise above the belief in error. Driven by his fanaticism and his spirit of intolerance, this prophet distinguished himself by untimely violence against the prophets of Baal. But faced with the fury of Jezebel, he could not contain his fear, until the Truth showed him the need to climb the mountain, to rise above the error, because it is only in the quiet that the small voice of truth is heard. Having reached the top of the celestial inspiration, Elijah learned that God does not use the violent ways of the human will.

Sixteen years ago, I had an experience that demonstrates the need to keep hope in adversity. In fact we were digging a hole to repair an underground pipe. The hole had reached a depth of 3 meters and I was in it thinking how to fix the pipe when there was landslide. In the blink of an eye, I was completely buried; only the right hand and the hair were visible, but a second landslide made the hair disappear underground. The first thought that came to me was not to be afraid. My nephew, who was the only witness of the scene, ran to get help. And meanwhile, I distinctly heard a suggestion of fear of death coming to my mind. I pushed it, I turned my attention to God and I began to pray the Lord's Payer[29] meditating deeply the words. I was calm and confident in the omnipotence of divine Love. After 30 minutes they dug me safe.

---

[29] Voir *Mathieu* 6: 9-13.

In any situation of adversity, we must refuse to let us embark in fear and turn our attention to the divine inspirations. Armed with the conviction of the divine omnipotence, we must rise above error understanding that evil is only a suggestion coming to our thinking, a suggestion that we can and must reject through the power the Word, the Christ.

8. AFROCENTRIC TRINITY

The Black African concept of trinity is as old as the untold story of this continent. This notion goes back to the conception of Egyptian deities who were represented in married couple with a child.

Since time immemorial, trinity has always modulated the daily life of the African. The week, of many African ethnics for example, has traditionally four days; thus some Africans worked for three days and rested the fourth. Three is the number of perfection for the Black-African thought.

As the Egyptians claimed a celestial origin of their kingdom from the trinitarian Gods, it is not excluded that the African kingdoms saw their past with the same features. The Bakongo, for example, argue that they are descendants of the three children N'Zinga, each representing one of the gods of the heavenly trinity NZAMBI Ampûngu Tulêndo (God Most

High), Mbumba Lowa (God the creator) and Mpina Nza (God the governor of humanity). Trinity was a fundamental principle upon which the Kongo society was conceived; as explained in the wisdom of the descendant of N'Zinga *"Makukua matatu malamba Kongo."* (This means: Kongo is a pot standing on three stones.)

Afrocentric trinity is quite different from scholastic trinity. It involves the unity of the Father-Mother, the Child and the Word, in substance, activity and existence. Trinity is seen in Black African deep spirituality, as eternal and temporal.

On the eternal plan: Trinity is the unity of God Almighty, the Child (all the Children of God represented by the Creator God) and the Word (God the judge or the governor) in the destiny of eternity. The Father-Mother is the source of all existence, He is Life. The Child is the manifestation of the true nature of the Father-Mother; so he is the Truth. The Word manifests all the goodness of the Father-Mother in each Child and around each Child. Thus trinity is the expression of Life, Truth and Love.

Temporally, trinity is the unity of the Father-Mother (God the Creator), the Child (you and me) and the Word (represented by the first man created male and female and having dominion over all the earth). In Kongo tradition the Word on the temporal plan is Kimahungu and the original man is called Mahungu. The original man, that René Garliet calls "the eldest Son of Heaven and Earth"[30] is designated in

---

[30] René Garliet , *les Maitres de la brousse*, Grue Couronnée, Kinshasa, 1976,

the Gabonese Eboga by name Mbandji. Speaking of the Word in the temporal plan Garliet says: "For many Africans, [the eldest Child of Heaven and Earth, the Word] summarizes, in unity, the essential forces of nature and manifests himself as the receptacle of the vital breath." This perfect nature of being is present in every man, that's why the Bantu (and several other ethnics including the Ijaw of Nigeria) call their right part male and the left female; thus every human being is essentially male and female, as claimed by the Bambara.

The temporal notion of the Word, as recorded in the Bible in Genesis (I: 226-27), where man is created male and female and has dominion over all the earth, become in Christianity the concept of Christ the fullness of being that animated Jesus and which is present in every man.

To better understand trinity in the temporal plan, figurate yourself as being in front of a mirror, so you face three realities: your presence in front of the mirror, your reflection in the mirror and the power of optical reflection. All you do is reproduced by the image through the power of reflection, and all that your image does manifests your activity through the power of reflection. You, your image in the mirror and the power of reflection form a temporal inseparable trinity, in the substance, the existence and activity. In this analogy, you symbolize the Father-Mother, the image symbolizes the Child (every child of God), and the power of optical reflection symbolizes the Word, the power of spiritual reflection.

---

p. 39.

Understanding this trinity Jesus said, "Verily, verily, I say unto you, The Son can do nothing of himself, he does what he sees the Father doing; and whatever the Father does, the Son does likewise." (John 5: 19).

Thus the Father-Mother always acts through a Child. When we pray, it is always a Child (who is in heavens) who meets our needs in the name of the Father-Mother who is in heaven. The heavens are different from the heaven by being temporal (see 2 Peter 3: 10), while the heaven is eternal. Jesus understanding that the Father-Mother acts always by a Child, always addressed his prayers to the "Father who is in heavens", and this Father answered him in the name of the Father-Mother who is eternally in heaven.

God is light and in Him there is no darkness at all. He therefore sees no illusions called disease, sin and death. God meets our needs not by knowing our difficulties, but by being all in us and around us; God makes the Word, the manifestation of His goodness, be eternally with us, and by this constant presence of His love, He answers all our needs without even knowing them.

Afrocentric trinity also implies that the Child (you and me) can in reality do only what the Father-Mother does in Him, because he is inseparable from the Father-Mother in the acting. The Bible expresses this truth by saying in Philippians 2: 13: "it is God which worketh in you both to will and to do of his good pleasure."

I still remember the day at the University the professor of philosophy gave me the rating 2/20. All my friends were convinced that rating did not reflect my application in this course and advised me to talk to the teacher. Rather than talk

65

with this philosopher, I chose to apply my understanding of Afrocentric trinity, because I knew the professor, as the child of God was inseparable from his Father-Mother, and therefore, it is God alone who acts in him. The conviction that it is God alone who acts in the professor had awakened the consciousness of this later; without my intervention he decided to revise my rating upwards.

Scholastic theology has changed the concept of the trinity in an incongruous henotheistic vision. But the high Black African spirituality allows us to understand that trinity is the unity of the Father-Mother, the Child of God and the Word, in the substance, the existence and activity. This practical trinity teaches us that the Father-Mother acts always through the Child who is in heavens, through the Word, for the benefit of the child who seems to be on the earth. The understanding of trinity gives strength to our actions and brings us closer to the day when, in our everyday experience, the Child (every child of God) will always do the Father-Mother's will.

9. PRAYER AND PURIFICATION

The history and the spiritual tradition teach us that the Afrocentric divine mystery is based on the path of the Word, the presence and manifestation of God's activity in and around man. The concept of the Word is the center and circumference of the art of the practice of Afrocentric intercession. This concept is first perceived by Africans as the manifestation of the divine perfection; perfection symbolized by the manifestation of paternal maternal natures of God. The Word as the fullness of being is symbolized by the conjunction of male and female nature in the being.

To express the fact that the Word, the divine perfection of being is inseparable from man, the Bantu commonly call the right side of their body male and the left female. The real man being thus male and female always reflects the divine perfection, the wholeness of being; he is the image and likeness of God. The Bible agrees with this vision of being because it shows us in Genesis 1: 27-28, that man in the image and likeness of God was created male and female, and to him was given dominion over all the earth. Thus, in the Bible, from Genesis, this notion of wholeness of being is rendered as the notion of the Christ: "For in Him dwells all the fullness of divinity."[31]

However the African divine mystery shows us that due to his disobedience, man seems to have lost the perfect condition of his being, his dominion over nature. Thus the religious practice of the Black-man tries to help man realize that this perfect nature of being, the Word, is always present in him and around him. The natural process of Afrocentric divine mystery in this research is the purification of the thought; the practice of Afrocentric spirituality is above all an art of purification.

Purity was always regarded in Africa as the cornerstone of the uplifting of being in the heavenly hierarchy. All the devotion of the Black-Africans consists therefore above all in the acceptance of the presence of the Word in us and in living it in daily life through sanctification. This enables us to experience the presence of the Word around ourselves; this implies the fact of finding ourselves among the pure ones who have preceded us in the Hereafter; because as the saying goes, "similar flock."

This purification of thought has always been symbolized by our ancestors by water. The saint-ancestors are said to abide in the water, not physically, but spiritually. Afrocentric spirituality

---

[31] *Colossiens* 2: 9.-

teaches us that those who, like the saint-ancestors, accept the Word, the divine nature or Christ, live in holiness of thought and are also in the water and try to reach the state of being free from any belief of pleasure in the flesh which is symbolized by the air.

Today the science of Afrocentric devotion shows us that the art of purification is not ritual, but is a demonstration of God's grace working through the Word. Man does not become pure, but become aware and agrees that, through God, he has always been pure, he is and always will be. The realization of this inherent purity of being is not a license that gives free rein to sin because it involves the realization that sin never had real power to do us good.

When a student commits a mathematical mistake in calculation, his first step forward is to recognize his mistake. The student who recognizes his error is a good future mathematician as he is in the way of applying the rule correctly to arrive to the right solution. So whoever, starting from the basis that man created in the image of God is always pure, acknowledges his sin, is a good believer to the extent that he can apply the spiritual rule by realizing that sin did him no good, and by committing himself to move forward. The alleged power of sin and its hold on man therefore lies in the belief that sin has done us good, or can do us good.

To recognize sin is in no way to see oneself as a mortal sinner, but rather to expose the assumption that sin has power over us, to recognize and reject the suggestion that sin had and will have power to do good. Afrocentric trinity teaches us that the Father-Mother, the Child (you and me) and the Word are inseparable in their substance, existence and activity. The

70

Child is the perfect manifestation of the Father-Mother's nature. So is God our purity, He has always been and always will be so. Always manifesting the purity of the Father-Mother, the Child is always pure; hence sin has never really had the power to do us good and never will. The belief of pleasure in sin, one of the sources of the bondage of humanity, never thus has real grip on us.

But we really made a step in repentance to the extent we have passed the point where we were before. In other words, the realization that there is no pleasure in sin should lead us to leave sin behind us, or at least take a step beyond our current position. It does not matter that we still fall into sin, as far as the realization of the emptiness of sin is sincere and as our commitment to move forward is practical, we are moving to the point where sin will disappear from our consciousness.

The realization of the purity of being is an essential step in the Afrocentric devotion; it allows man to become more clearly aware of the presence of the saint-ancestors around him; because, ultimately, to pray in the Afrocentric spiritual tradition, it to present ones case to the "spirits of just men made perfect."[32] The presence of the saint-ancestors, symbolizes the presence of the Word around man.

Since the art of Afrocentric intercession consists in pleading ones case to the "spirits of just men made perfect", purification is an essential element. But far from being confined to purification rites, it is the elevation of thought, by

_____

[32] *Hébreux* 12: 23.

the realization of the inherent purity of being and the realization that sin never had a real power to do us good; because man is actually inseparable from the Word, the presence, manifestation and activity of God in man and around man.

10. PRAISE BELONGS TO THE ALMIGHTY

From time immemorial, music and dance have always accompanied the worship of the Almighty God by the African. African art had primarily a spiritual function, for God was always at the center of the cultural activity of the Black-man.

Even today, every Sunday, the sounds of drums, or modern orchestras, are heard in almost every street of the city of Kinshasa, where I live. This is music that marks the worship services, a prelude to any service in the New Born Churches that abound in the town: by a music punctuated with dances and shouting, the believers praise the Lord.

However, the Afrocentric spiritual culture does not fail to emphasize that God is Spirit. The African thus knows, deep within him, that true worship is spiritual. Seeking to illustrate this point to me an old lady, initiated of the Kimpasi, one of the Kongo initiatory schools, made me understand that the highest form of prayer is to be in the presence of God and his army of saints without saying anything, without even saying a word mentally, but just staying in deep contemplation of the glory of God.

We can praise God through music and dance, but we must mostly praise Him by a spiritualized consciousness, through a thought elevated by the contemplation of His infinite glory. To praise God in the highest degree, is thus to be aware of His nature.

To help humanity gain a higher meaning of the nature of the Supreme Being, the Divine Science depicts His divinity through His seven synonymous. These synonyms are mentioned in the Afrocentric spirituality in several ways: the prophet Simon Kimbangu speaks of seven angels who rule in the court of the Almighty God.[33] The great Egyptian priest Thoth speaks of seven heavens, each of which is a light that flows toward our humanity to get us completely out of darkness.

The seven synonyms of God are: Life, Truth, Love, Principle, Mind, Soul and Spirit. Being synonymous, these seven names refer to the same being: God. They are interchangeable, although each defines a particular aspect of God's nature. A building can have many entries, but each of them gives access to the same building and provides a particular aspect of it. So is it with the seven synonyms of

---

[33] Cf., Kiatezua Lubanzadio Luyaluka, *la Religion Kongo*, Paris: l'Harmattan, 2010, p. 149.

God. Each synonym gives a particular perspective of the ministry and nature of God.

Let me illustrate my point with a short example. One day I arrived at the architecture school I attended, I was greeted by loud noises coming from upstairs. I was told that my fellow students were in a room since four hours discussing about the continuation or cessation of a strike, boycott of classes, which had finally fallen into deadlock, the authorities having so far taken no action to satisfy the grievances of the students who were protesting against the arbitrariness in the management of academic activities. Rather than join in the discussion, I decided to pray to resolve the situation.

My prayer consisted in praising God through the synonymous Principle; the ministry of God as Principle is to rule the universe by His spiritual laws. This understanding naturally led me to deny the arbitrariness and injustice that seemed to be the norm in the decisions of teachers. After arguing for about five minutes that the divine Principle alone governs this school of architecture in a fair, orderly, harmonious and perfect manner; through truth and love, I denied any suggestion of injustice and arbitrariness in the conduct of the school. As I was praying, I heard a loud noise; I was told that the students had decided, in a mutual agreement, to end the strike. A few days later, the academic authorities decided to base their decisions on specific set of laws they announced to all students. No more arbitrary decisions!

The synonymous Principle shines in all other synonymous; it is symbolized by the central stem of the pure-gold lamp-stand of the Israelite tabernacle, each stem of the lamp-stand (always curved) represents one of the seven heavens. Each synonym is somehow the Principle, or the individual source of the attributes of divinity.

Mind is the source of ideas, the Principle of memorization. The Ministry of Mind is to supply man with ideas, in a manner clear, logical, intelligent, without any forgetting, etc. Thus man can in reality neither issue nor receive erroneous suggestions, because God is the only Mind. The term mind refers to man's spiritual sense of memorizing. Man, being spiritual, does not retain thoughts through his brain, although it symbolizes his infinite memorizing capacity.

Soul, the divine consciousness, is the Principle of perception, of will, volition, desire, individuality and feeling; Soul is the source of everything that pleases the spiritual sense. As a source of spiritual sensations, Soul can arouse in us only His own infinite, perfect, ennobling sensations, full of inspiration, and not the physical sensations; the sensations of Soul tend to focus our awareness on our infinite irradiation of infinite spiritual qualities. Speaking of Soul, the Bible says: "It is God which worketh in you both to will and to do of his good pleasure."[34] The joys that material sensations pretend to give us are always in reality opposed to the true happiness that derives from the "good pleasure" of Soul. The ministry of Soul is to will, to desire in his idea, man. Thus man can really desire only what is of the divine nature. Soul individualizes His ideas. The term soul, in divine metaphysics, is the spiritual sense or

---

[34] Philippiens 2: 13.

the ability of man to will, to desire. The attributes of Soul include joy, peace, glory, splendor, harmony…

Spirit is the substance of being as a manifestation of all spiritual qualities. Spirit is the principle which animates being. Since God, Spirit, is all, matter, as substance, does not exist. A plane in the sky seems very small. But thanks to a higher sense of perception, we say that the plane is actually big, i.e., where a small plane seems to hover, there is actually only one plane: the big.

Similarly, to the human sense, man and the universe appear to be limited, material. But, using the spiritual sense, we can realize that even now man and the universe are infinite, spiritual; they are formed of infinite qualities. Where we seem to see finite muscles, we use our spiritual senses to perceive infinite power. Where there seems to be a limited material heart, we can realize the infinite goodness. Where man appears to have two limited eyes, we can see that vision is infinite. Man is totally spiritual; he is composed of limitless qualities. Matter is a limited and reversed way of seeing reality which is even now spiritual.

The ministry of Spirit is to give identity (all spiritual qualities) to each of His ideas, to animate each of His ideas. Spirit is indivisible, infinite, perfect, unlimited, etc.

The term spirit in the divine metaphysics refers to spiritual sense or the ability to perceive that man has. It is the soul in man that looks, but it is the spirit which sees; it is the soul of man which listens, but it is the spirit which hears. The soul is what in us seeks to understand, to perceive, to enjoy, etc. But it is the spirit in us which really understand, perceive, enjoy, etc. The corporeal senses claim to help man understand, perceive and enjoy, but they are usurpers who seek to assume the rights of the spirit. The corporeal senses are limited and inaccurate in their perceptions and dispensations, the dispensations of the spirit alone bring to man real satisfaction.

Life is the Principle of being, of its unfolding and its activity. Life is the Principle of eternity. Life is without beginning or end. The ministry of Life is to express the existence, unfolding, activity and infinite good in man and the universe. The attributes of Life are: eternity, immortality, abundance, activity, etc.; thus, birth, death, inactivity, unemployment, underdevelopment, etc., are all opposites of Life. Man must therefore deny them access to his conscience, for his life, his ability to manifest spiritual existence is infinite.

Truth is the principle of reality; the source of the perfection of man and the universe. The ministry of Truth is to express and maintain the spiritual fact (the perfection of being) in man and the universe. Sin, sickness and death are contrary to the spiritual fact of being; so these are errors that Truth destroys by the activity of the Word, the manifestation, the presence and the activity of God in man and around man. Attributes of Truth are sincerity, invariability, uprightness, honesty, etc.

Love is the Principle of goodness. The ministry of Love is to express the goodness of God in man and the universe. Knowing that a man is always governed by love, we should deny hatred and personnel attachment, which are opposite of Love. Divine Love is impartial, universal, loving, pure, tender, etc. The word love actually refers to the ability of man to manifest the divine goodness.

Each of the seven synonyms helps us to give glory to God. In our prayers, we can affirm the ministry of God in an exclusive way through all His attributes and deny everything that is contrary to the spiritual facts of being.

We can all become better healers in improving our understanding of God through a proper understanding of His synonymous. Understanding that the attributes are our true being will help us realize the presence and power of God and to deny all claims of sin, sickness and death; because these lies are contrary to God's nature. And the realization of this fact is a true and high praise befitting to the Almighty.

11. 50 YEARS AFTER THE INDEPENDENCES

Seated in a chair, I was watching on TV one day the presentation of a logo designed for the celebration of 50 years of independence of the Democratic Republic of Congo (DRC). The fever of preparation for the celebration of the fiftieth anniversary is not only the case of the great nation of the heart of Africa, if we remember that most African independences were acquired in the 1960s. This celebration of fiftieth anniversary of independences call to mind several questions, among others: in fifty years of independence did our African nations make progress? It is therefore right that the Congolese scientists are called upon to reflect on the positive and negative aspects of our journey during the fifty years of independence and to propose solutions for the future.

It is certain that called to give an opinion on the evolution of Africa during the past fifty years; the views can only be diverse and even divergent. While the picture is not entirely negative, as a noted scientist in the DRC by asking the following question at a conference on the fiftieth anniversary of independence: "In 1960, the DRC had about 400 students finalists of the secondary school, for the ending year it has counted more than 400,000. So should we say that there has been progress or not?"

Given the multitude of interventions that seek to lean to such position or another, I would rather ask this question: is it not wise to first ask ourselves what was (or is) the dependence, in order to show in an informed way whether our independences have brought the fruits that we should expect.

To speak of dependence is first of all to ask: when did it start? It is easy to think of the beginning of the dependence as the beginning of colonization. But in fact dependence is actually more than political. Its roots must be sought in the inoculation of a mentality that tends to almost render the African a marionette without identity who only apes the White. Thus it is at the meeting of the West and Africa that we must go to find the beginning and the nature of the dependence, i.e., at the discovery in the fifteenth century of the Kingdom of Kongo by the Portugal, the then superpower.

When the Portuguese navigator Diego Cao reaches the Kingdom of Kongo for the first time on April 23 in 1482, he is surprised to discover a prosperous kingdom with well-organized institutions, a kingdom where people lived in peace, while during the same time, despite their technical and military superiority, Europeans lived in a terror of witchcraft; so it was the time of the witch hunt. As Schaff says: "In the second half of that century, the Church and society were thrown into a panic over witchcraft, and Christendom seemed to be suddenly infested with a great company of bewitched people, who yielded themselves to the irresistible discipline of Satan."[35]

In this Europe, where manufacturing was booming, nothing delighted more the White man than gold mines and cheap labor that could be taken from "ebony" (hear slaves) mines.

Material interests taking precedence, the relationship between the Kingdom of Kongo and Portugal will be calculated in the proportions of a need to exploit a nation dazzled by material possessions of the Westerners. Capitalizing on their economic and technological superiority and intolerance, blinded by the spirit of the Inquisition which saw in any culture different from Christianity nothing but paganism, the Westerners conceived that it was their duty to bring the Truth to the Black-man and especially to draw him out of the "darkness" in which they saw him plunged.

Evangelism has been undertaken in Africa with as accompanying elements: the exportation of fear of witchcraft (which characterized the darkened atmosphere of Europe at that time) and prejudices about the inferiority and the pagan nature of the Black African spirituality.

Meanwhile, no one has bothered to understand the reason of the prosperity of the Kingdom of Kongo, or at least having understood it malicious souls were rather trying to scuttle it. Spirituality underlay everything in this African kingdom. The country owed its prosperity to the system of socio-theocratic democracy where the divine spirituality served as a safeguard against the misuse of human power by the masses and against any use of demonic forces.

---

[35] Schaff, P., *History of the Christian church*, http://ccel.wheaton.edu, html

Clearly there was in the Kongo spiritual system a highly divine religion where spiritual elevation was obtained by the purification of thought, a religion that spread knowledge that might be called the Kongo divine mystery, the high Kongo initiatory science that the indigenous themselves called *kindoki* (do not rush to confuse it with witchcraft[36]). This *kindoki* was taught in well structured initiatory academies, whose priesthood taught, not disparate doctrines, but a unified teaching, as was always recommend by Kongo wisdom: "*Tuvuka mpându, ka tuvambundi mpându ko.*" (In the rituals, which stand figuratively for doctrines, let's be united.)

Besides the divine mystery (the divine *kindoki*), there was also the human mystery. This mystery, which included the majority of the Kongo population, spread a teaching where power was acquired by human means and this power can be used for good or evil purposes. This is the equivalent of the education provided by our modern schools and universities. As for the divine mystery, the teachings of human *kindoki* were delivered in diversified initiatory institutions over the entire kingdom.

The academies of the divine and human mystery were the only formal educational institutions in the Kingdom of Kongo. However, as on the temporal plan human society faces the incursions of the devil, there was a third mystery

---

[36] I demonstrate the difference between the *kindoki* and witchcraft in my book titled: *Vaincre la sorcellerie en Afrique*, (Paris: Harmattan, 2009), see pp. 80-85. The original version of this book was published under the pseudonym of Ne Kiana Mazamba and was titled: *Kindoki: an African Mystery Elucidated.*

which was only the depravation of the human mystery, the demonic mystery. Unlike the divine *kindoki* in the demonic *kindoki* the power was obtained by the corruption of thought or through demonic spirits. This mystery could thus be used only for evil. In other words, the demonic *kindoki* necessarily led to witchcraft (the use of evil forces in order to harm).

To what thing was due the progress of this socio-theocratic democracy which is the Kingdom of Kongo? It is in the grip of the highest divine spirituality that we must seek the explanation of this progress. The progress of the Kingdom of Kongo was therefore the result of effective control of the divine mystery on the human mystery, which controls required of those engaged in the human *kindoki* to use their power for good purposes only. Unfortunately this aspect of things eludes historians and modern scientific analysts. Human *kindoki* (the power of the majority of the population) is as taken between two opposing forces: the divine *kindoki* and the demonic *kindoki*. The supremacy of the first leads to progress, while the influence of the second implies an inevitable decline.

At the arrival of Westerners, the Kongo initiatory system was healthy and the divine *kindoki* by its teachings, its wisdom and its prayers maintained the human *kindoki* in a constructive way; this explained the peace and prosperity enjoyed by the Kingdom of Kongo. Christian evangelism had as unfortunate corollary the destruction of the grip of the divine mystery on the human mystery.

Christian evangelism, as I said above, was accompanied by an export of the fear of witchcraft prevailing in Europe and the prejudice that brought Europeans to believe themselves spiritually superior to Blacks. Professor Matukanga emphasizes this state of affairs when he writes: "According to the missionaries of the first evangelism, the Kongo culture was demonic. And everything that had to do with it was diabolical. For F. Fra Luca da Caltanissetta, the fetishists were the priests of the devil.

"The care provided by them was evil, the polygamous entertained diabolical relationships with many women, and the secret society Kimpasi was a cult of the devil. As writes P. Bontinck: "prisoner of his time, Fra Luca saw only diabolic superstitions in the paganism in the milieu of which he lived for twelve years; the epithet 'evil' is the one occurring most frequently in his writings.

"The report of F. Zenobio Da Firenze returns again on it and insists on the superstitious rites of Kongo."[37]

The unfortunate consequence of this negative vision of Kongo spirituality was naturally:

- The demonization of the entire Kongo spiritual culture. Which will lead the Church to teach the Blacks that *kindoki* (initiatory teaching and the power it confers) is equal to witchcraft. Erroneous conclusion that inevitably will cause the destruction of the influence of the divine mystery on the human one.

---

[37] Matukanga, « Ambigüité de la néoculture Kongo ? », in *500 ans d'évangélisation et de rencontre des cultures en pays Kongo*, Kisantu, 1996, pp. 130 & &131

- The destruction of the influence of the divine mystery on the human. This had as direct consequence the influence of demonic mystery on the human mystery; which will result in the destruction of peace and prosperity enjoyed by the Kingdom of Kongo. For the Church, not understanding what African witchcraft is and what actually is *kindoki*, fails to take over the role of the divine *kindoki* in the control of human mystery and the defeating the demonic mystery.[38]

- The separation of the Kongo man from the support of his ancestors who were the enlightened indispensable intermediaries between the living and the Most High God, Nzambi Ampûngu Tulêndo.

- The abandonment of *animic* technology[39], the result of the deductive thinking that characterized Black African

---

[38] An article titled *Witchcraft destroying the Catholic Church in Africa, experts say*, corroborates this conclusion, it can be read on: http://www.catholic.org/printer_friendly.php?id=22994&section=Cathco m.

[39] Regarding this technology, Kimpianga Mahania writes: « the political chiefs (*mfumu*), the medico-ritual priests (*banganga*), the seers (*ngunza*) and the blacksmith (*ngangula*) used the *kindoki* to heal, to invent the necessary techniques that can ensure the material and psychological conditions in which us evolve the individual and the community." (*La Problématique crocodilienne à Luozi*, CVA, Kinshasa, 1989, p. 31.)

lore, in favor of the Western technology fruit of an essentially inductive thinking.

So from the perspective of all this development, the dependence which was (and still is) the fate of Africa had essentially as bases:

- The destruction of African divine mystery, the divine spirituality taught and lived by Africans before the arrival of Westerners.

- The breaking of the link between the African and his illuminated-ancestors.

- The rise of witchcraft and the inability of the Church to curb this scourge.

- The abandonment by the African of his deductive original epistemology in which intuition has supremacy over reason.

Fifty years after the independences, we must ask ourselves: Do we have eradicated the root causes of the dependence? In fact the current situation of the Black continent rather demonstrates that Africans compete mainly to eradicate the consequences instead of addressing the root causes of dependence. Viable solutions to the African problems can only be found through the contribution of spirituality and philosophy in solving these four key issues that underlie the dependence still affecting Africa.

12. PRAYER THAT DEFEATS EFFICIENTLY WITCHCRAFT

Witchcraft is one of the beliefs man has to face daily in Africa; to know how to fight efficiently this plague is thus a pressing need there. In the research of the ways and means to fight efficiently this plague, one of the great difficulties is the bad idea that people entertain of this concept. Witchcraft is primarily a malefic practice, thus it should not be confused with the spiritual traditions of Africa which were intended primarily for good purposes.

In my book titled *Vaincre la sorcellerie en Afrique*[40], I show the difference which exists between the African spiritual practices and witchcraft. Africa had official setting for teaching Spirituality, and the aim of teaching spirituality was the development of the metaphysical faculties of being. While witchcraft has always been a practice condemned by society and its goal has always been primarily to harm. Witchcraft is an erroneous use of spirituality and metaphysical potential. This comprehension is essential, for those who work to fight witchcraft through prayer, because due to the lack of it, they

---

[40] Kiatezua Lubanzadio Luyaluka, *Vaincre la sorcellerie en Afrique*, Paris: L'Harmattan, 2009.

rather work to destroy the good and the evil in the African cultures.

During one of my trip in my career of lecturer, I went to Haiti in the city of Désarmes to publicly speak about the nothingness of witchcraft. More than two hundred people came to listen to me on the manner of efficiently fighting witchcraft by the prayer. I know by experience that when one speaks publicly against this dark practice, he exposes himself to the attacks coming on behalf of those who cling to it.

Everything went very well, but after the lecture, I started to feel pains in my belly. I was to be next day on my way back to Boston via Miami, Florida. While I was at the airport of Miami, the bellyache accentuated; I was victim of an attack by witchcraft. The mental atmosphere in Haiti is very similar to that which one feels in African milieus; witchcraft is also confused there with spirituality in the voodoo. I thus had an opportunity to prove that the ideas that I had shared with my Haitian brothers were practical and efficient in the fight against witchcraft.

- My first stage was to become aware of my purity as a child of God. Purification always has been the prelude to any efficient prayer in the highest African spirituality. Our ancestors sometimes practiced ablution rituals before their prayers, because water in Africa has always been a symbol of purity. Although getting inspiration from their approach, I do not spouse a ritualistic vision of spirituality. I always understand purification as an assertion of one's purity in the present, the past and the future, by starting from the basis that man is now the image and likeness of God and that sin never had the power to one any good.

This understanding has always enabled me to see more clearly that sin does not have the power to separate me from God, because the power of the sin and its influence on the man lies only in the belief that it has a real power to do him good.

To affirm our purity as children of God is also a way of affirming the presence of Christ (the divine Word) in us. Divine science shows us that the divine Word is the perfect presence of God in the man and around man (See the article on the Christ). In Bantu devotional practice, this double nature of the Word is essential to prayer, because God in heaven answers our prayers through the Father-Mother which is the heavens via the Word, the Christ.

The biblical book of the Revelation (in chapter 19) shows us that Christ is the commander of the armies of heavens; he thus leads all the army of the saints. It is through this army of the saints that God answers our prayers and it is through it that our ancestors addressed their prayers to God the Almighty. Because they knew that a commander does not fight himself but uses his troops. And to help me, the commander, the divine Word, could only use the troops which are closest to me and which know my problem better, i.e. my saint-ancestors.

The efficient prayer thus requires of man that he realizes his purity to approach the Christ, however to approach Christ is to approach his army of saints; thus prayer implies the fact of approaching the saint-ancestors by the way of the purification of thought. I also knew that nothing can resist the army of Christ, the army of the saints.

After having affirmed my purity and having realized the presence of the army of saints around me, I exposed to the court of heavens, to the court of the saints, my desire to see myself released of this alleged influence of witchcraft on my being. Bantus always perceived prayer to be like the fact of pleading one's cause in front of the celestial judges; in several Bantus languages the same word is used to say "to pray" and to say "to plead in front of a court". The Bible shows us the same vision of prayer when Christ enjoins us: "Come now, let us argue it out, says the Lord." (Isaiah 1: 18 *the New Oxford Annotated Bible.*)

Having exposed my case to the celestial court of Christ, i.e., having made my petition to "the spirits of just men made perfect"[41], the saint-ancestors, I started to argue against the belief in witchcraft as I had taught it to the crowd that came to listen to me in Désarmes. My argumentation consisted in affirming the nothingness of witchcraft.

The force of witchcraft is first of all the belief in the spirits. The witch claims to act as a spirit or he claims to be controlled by spirits. But, the only true spirit is God, and I know that He alone controls me and controls everyone including those who seem to attack me. Only the spirit of Truth and divine Love controls man, thus nobody does have the real ability to harm his neighbor. With this understanding, next I realized the fact that God is the real source of very true thought. The Bible

---

[41] The author of the Epistle to the Hebrew shows us that when one is purified he is on a spiritual mountain in front of saint-ancestors ("the spirits of just men made perfect") (Hebrew 12: 22-24)

says: "For it is God which worketh in you both to will and to do of his good pleasure." (Phil. 2: 13) Thus, I could be neither transmitter nor receiver of the aggressive suggestions. I affirmed that this was known in all the city of Désarmes, because God knows it in each one of us, that the evil which one does to others reacts violently against himself and that nobody could attack me, because witchcraft carries the witch surely to death right now; hence the witches have no other alternatives but to give up. This realization was the activity of the divine grace in me working for the salvation of those who let the evil govern them. It was thus first of all an act of love. The efficient prayer does not consist in attacking the witch, but witchcraft; however witchcraft will be overcome only insofar as we help the witches to leave the dark practice and the means of doing it is to ask the Father-Mother to show them the consequence of their action: death.

With this conviction of the nothingness of witchcraft, I maintained in my conscience, during all this night at the airport of Miami, that the suggestion of bellyache (because whatever its nature, evil is always a suggestion, it is never a presence nor a belief in us) did not have any influence on me, nor on anyone, because God has all power and He is all-presence; all that exists really manifests His power and His presence. I also realized that this suggestion could not even actually exist, because God is the only Mind.

The rays of the sun announcing a new day through the large glass-windows of the airport, brought me the joy of realizing that day that my lecture on the nothingness of witchcraft at Désarmes was practical, because I was completely healed of this bellyache which claimed to overmaster me.

The prayer that realizes the purity of man and his unity with Christ, i.e., with its army of the saints, is an efficient asset to overcome witchcraft, insofar as it enables us to realize that God is the only Spirit which controls us and which thinks in us and that nobody can practice witchcraft without punishment.

13. CHRIST IN BANTU SPIRITUAL TRADITION AND IN CHRISTIAN SCIENCE

13.1. Introduction

The notion of the divine Word is often not well understood and we generally tend to believe that it is exclusive to the Christian religion. However this notion of the divine Word is the angular stone of the Bantu's high spiritual tradition: the divine spiritual tradition. We will elucidate in this article the notion of the divine Word in accordance with the Bantu initiatory tradition and to Christian Science as taught by Mary Baker Eddy.

13.2. The divine Word in the African spiritual tradition

The Bakongo[42] taught, well before the arrival of the white man in Africa, that the first human being created by God was both male and female and had the dominion over all the earth. But due to disobedience, he lost his divine nature and found himself divided into two beings: a man and a woman. However Mahungu (the original man) actually did not lose his divine nature, he simply lost sight of it; because this nature is still in each one of us. Therefore, the majority of the Bantus call their right part the male part and their left part the female; thus symbolizing the presence in them of this complete nature of being.

---

[42] Members of the Kongo ethnic who are found in Angola and in both Congos.

This complete nature of being, whereby man is male and female and have dominion over all, is the divine Word or Christ. Speaking of this complete nature of being Jesus says in the Bible: "For it pleased the Father that in him should all fullness dwell." (I Colossians 1: 19)

In Lemba, one of the Kongo initiatory schools, it was recommended to the initiate: "*'Bôka kua mûntu walunga'* or call upon the complete man."[43] That means invoke the complete nature of being or the Christ. The Bakongo thus knew that prayer must be addressed to Christ, i.e., through the ideal man, or to the ideal men and not to mortals.

13.3.   The Christ in the Bantu trinity

The notion of trinity was not unknown of Bantus. One finds it in Kongo spiritual tradition as well as in the administrative and social organization of the Kingdom of Kongo. Trinity in Kongo tradition implies:

- The unity of the Father-Mother, the Child and the Word on the celestial eternal plan:

  o Nzâmbi Ampûngu Tulêndo, the source of all existence.

  o Mbumba Lowa, representing the Children of God on the celestial plane.

---

[43] Fukiau, A., *le Mukôngo et le monde qui l'entourait*, Kinshasa, 1969, p.113

- o Mpina Nza, the divine Word, God governor of humanity.

- • The unity of the Father-Mother, the Child and the Word in the destiny of the terrestrial man.

- o Mbumba Lowa, Creator God.

- o Mahungu, the true Child of God.

- o Kimahungu, Christ, the power that enables man to be a Child of God.

We also know that in the Lemba of Doualas (the initiatory spiritual tradition of the Doualas of Cameroun) the notion of trinity was taught, God is seen in this teaching manifested as:

- • Father-Mother: Nyangbé

- • Child: Kwa

- • Power: Dibenga

By analogy with Kongo trinity, one can conclude that in Douala's trinity Dibenga is the power that enables man to be Child (Kwa) of God.

This traditional doctrine of trinity is also found among the Mboshi, an ethnic group of the Republic of Congo. When the Mboshi refer to the trinity on the celestial plan they say:

- • Nzambe, Nzambe, Nzambe (God the Almighty is designated three times to convey His supreme and unutterable nature).

94

- Nzambe Iko-latsenge (God, the Creator of heavens and earth).

- Nzambe Kane (God the judge).

Trinity among the Bantus thus refers on the celestial plan to the divinity of the Father-Mother (God the Almighty), to the Child (the Creator of the temporal plans) and to God the judges or governor of humanity. While on the temporal level the Bantu trinity refers to the Father-Mother, to the ideal man (the Child) and to the power that enables man to become a perfect being.

13.4.   The double nature of Christ

After an analysis of the lesson of these African spiritual schools, we can say that the Africans already conceived the Christ as the divine childhood, the complete manifestation of God in man, the complete and perfect nature of being whereby man is male and female; i.e., whereby each one of us includes all male and female qualities of God; because "male and female" does not refer to the sex, but to the paternal and maternal nature of God.

Let us consider here one of the prayers of Bakongo's school of Lemba:

> Among those living in this plane,
> Among the ancestors,
> Bracelet and bracelet knock each other.
> Among those living in this plan,
> Among the ancestors,
> Eh Mahungu e!
> They gather around you.

The bracelet referred here was a distinctive sign of the initiates which symbolized their holiness;[44] because purity was a strong requirement in the traditional spiritual schools of the Bakongo. The knocking of these bracelets shows that every moment the initiates are always together; because this unity alone allows the knocking of their bracelet which they never put off.

In other words in this prayer the initiate was invited to realize the presence around him of the initiates who preceded him in the beyond. Whence the meaning of the following exclamation: "Eh Mahungu they gather around you." Note that the one called Mahungu here, or the perfect man, the complete man, or the Christ-man, is the disciple, the candidate to the initiation. And those who gather around him are the Masters who preceded him in the beyond, Christ-men; because they went through the same phases of purification as the disciple, they are thus Mahungu.

This brings us to a third vision that the African had of Christ. Christ for them is not only the complete nature of being in man, the son of God, but it is also the complete nature of being around man, symbolized by the presence of the complete beings around a complete being, the presence of the saints around a saint. Thus prayer for the Bantus consisted in becoming aware of the Christ in oneself, to become aware of Christ around oneself; in other words, to become aware of

---

[44] The Kongo term designating this bracelet is *n'lunga*, it comes from *lunga* which means to be complete; hence this bracelet symbolizes the perfect nature of being.

Christ-man in oneself in order to become aware of Christ-men around oneself. Hence Christ in this conception is the complete nature of being in man and around man.

13.5. The notion of man among the Bantus

The word man is translated into Bantus languages by *Muntu, Moto, Mutu, Mut, etc.* We know that these terms designate at the same time the human being and the head. But are these words really synonymous to the French word for man?

In all Bantus languages one can say of two *bato* (plural of *moto*) that they are a *moto*; however in French one cannot say of two men that they are a man, but rather than they are united. The French word for man refers to a corporeal being, while *muntu, moto,* or *mut,* refer to an idea, a consciousness. This consciousness can imply a human being, several human beings, or all the human beings. This rejoins the metaphysical concept that man is the idea of God and not a material corporeal being. Man in divine Science can thus be:

- Individual

- Collective

- Generic

13.6. Christ as the true idea of individual man

Christ, as a true idea of the individual man, implies the true nature of each one of us whereby each one includes all the qualities of God and does not lack anything. And in this true nature each one of us is a saint.

13.7.   Christ as the true idea of the collective man

If we consider an unspecified group of individuals, it constitutes a collective man, a set of individual men. Christ, as a true idea of this collective man, implies that each member of this group is a Christ-idea, that each individual idea in this group includes all the qualities of God. To affirm the Christ-nature of a family is thus to refuse to see in it imperfect mortals, but only, the pure, perfect and complete ideas of God.

13.8.   Christ as the true idea of the generic man

To understand that Christ is the true idea of the generic man is to understand that each man is even now a Christ-idea. Jesus was always conscious of the Christ as a true idea of the generic man, thus he healed easily. He constantly maintained the true idea of man, or the Christ-idea of man. We read in *Science and Health*: "Jesus beheld in Science the perfect man, who appeared to him where sinning mortal man appears to mortals. In this perfect man the Savior saw God's own likeness, and this correct view of man healed the sick." [45]

13.9.   Christ as ideal, message, idea, manifestation and nature

Beauty is a concept which is present in Mind (God as a source of ideas). The beauty in Mind is an ideal. God shares this ideal with us by a message, thus beauty is a message of

---

[45] Eddy, M. B., *Science et santé avec la clé des Ecritures*, Boston, 1875 p.476

Mind. Perceived by the human consciousness, this message becomes an idea. When this idea is understood and cherished in the consciousness, it appears on the body as a nature. *Beauty is thus at the same time an ideal, a message, an idea, a manifestation and finally a nature.* This can be said of all the ideas of God including the Christ.

- Christ is the divine ideal of man: Mary Baker Eddy writes: "Jesus presented the ideal of God better than could any man whose origin was less spiritual."[46]

- Christ as a message: we read in *Science and Health*: "Christ is the true idea voicing good, the divine message from God to men speaking to the human consciousness."[47]

- Christ is an idea: we read in *Science and Health*: "Christ is the true idea voicing good, (...)."[48]

- Christ is the manifestation of God: Mary Baker Eddy defines Christ this way in *Science and Health*: "The divine manifestation of God, which comes to the flesh to destroy incarnate error."[49]

---

[46] Ibidem p. 25

[47] Ibidem p. 332

[48] Ibidem p. 332

[49] Ibidem p. 583

- Christ is a nature: speaking about Christ as a nature Mary Baker Eddy says in *Science and a Health*: "This Christ, or divinity of the man Jesus, was his divine nature, the godliness which animated him."[50] She also says on page 119: "In one sense God is identical with nature, but this nature is spiritual and is not expressed in matter." And finally on page 333: 9, we read: "Christ expresses God's spiritual, eternal nature."*****

13.10. Jesus and the Christ

Christ is not, strictly speaking, the synonym of Jesus. We all know that on the political plan the notion of the president refers to the fact of governing a republican entity. But this word applied to Paul Biya (the president of Cameroon) becomes his title and designates also his personality as a Head of State. But Paul Biya and president are not synonyms.

Thus in connection to the personality of Jesus the term Christ refers to three concepts:

- The word Christ designates, strictly speaking, the divine idea of God, this idea that Jesus accepted and lived and that each one of us also must accept and live for his salvation.

- Christ is also the title of Jesus as a person who, at his time, had expressed the most the Christ.

---

[50] Ibidem p. 26

- Christ designates also the spiritual individuality of Jesus, the holiness that animated him and which healed the sick.

13.11. The notion holiness

Holiness implies the purity of the thoughts and acts. Holiness can be relative or absolute.

- **Holiness on the relative level**: A man can be purer than another, even though he has not yet developed all his holiness. A merchant, although using the belief in a personal human power to succeed in his trade by work, is holier than a brigand who kills to grow rich.

- **Holiness on the absolute level**: It is on the absolute plan that we use the term holy in connection with the Christ-idea. It is a nature of being whereby the belief of pleasure in sin is powerless and without influence on the being. This nature is the true manifestation of Christ in man; thus to become aware of Christ amounts to becoming aware of the holiness of God in us, this implies the fact of sanctifying one's being, becoming aware of one's purity, affirming and accepting in the bottom of heart that sin has never done us and will never do us any good.

Christ, holiness and the purity are thus three essentially linked concepts. Nobody can say that he realized the Christ when he did not become aware of his purity as a belief of pleasure in matter destroyed. And nobody can claim to have realized Christ in his neighbor, when he did not perceive in him the nothingness of the belief of the pleasure in sin, although this does not remove for the neighbor the need for working himself to accept the Christ, to reform. Understanding this, Jesus said to the adulteress: "go, and sin no more."[51] In other words although Jesus affirmed the Christ in her, it also belonged to her to accept the Christ in her own consciousness.

To become aware of Christ in us is to become aware of our absolute holiness and to endeavor to live it. To become aware of Christ around us is to become aware of the absolute holiness of the collective man or the generic man around us; it is to become aware of the presence of the saints around oneself.

13.12. Purity: the way toward the inner Christ

Purity is the only way which brings us to the demonstration of the Christ in us and to the perception of the Christ around us. It is essential to purify oneself to manifest the Christ in oneself and around oneself. But what does it means to purify oneself? We can read in *Science and Health*: "The great spiritual fact must be brought out that man is, not shall be, perfect and immortal."[52] To purify is thus to become aware that one was always pure and that one will be always be pure; it is not thus a question of becoming what one is not, but rather to prove what one always has been. This implies two things:

---

[51] *Jean* 8: 11

[52] Eddy, M. B. *Science et santé avec la clé des Ecritures*, Boston, 1875, p.428

102

- Purity does not depend on our acts, but our acts depend on purity.

- Purity is a gift of the Divine love, but it must be accepted; whoever accepts it must separate himself from sin, i.e., he must put away the belief of pleasure in sin.

The Pharisee who struck his chest while praying, claiming to be pure and not to be like the publican, believed that purity depends on his religious and humane acts. Thus his pride closed to him the entry in the kingdom of heavens, the conscience and the presence of Christ in him and around him.[53]

The publican who struck its chest in asking the leniency of the heavens towards him, made the same mistake than the Pharisee, because he believed that his purity depends on his acts and thus he condemned himself rather than condemn the sin, but contrary to the Pharisee, his humility enabled him to accept Christ and to live it.

We should adopt neither the position of the Pharisee nor that of the publican. We must rather recognize that sin is an evil and then become aware that sin never gave us any good, and thus it cannot separate us from our purity, but we must be consequent and commit ourselves to living this purity.

---

[53] Voir *Luc* 18: 10-14

13.13. Purification is not autosuggestion

It is important not to confuse the process of the purification with autosuggestion. We know that purification consists in becoming aware of one's purity as a child of God, in the past, the present and the future. But let us examine this concept a little more deeply.

We know that our ancestors considered prayer as being a lawsuit, in which man defends his cause in front of the heavens (i.e., in front of the saint-ancestors). For this reason in Douala, in Kikongo, and in Baoulé of Ivory Coast, the same word is used to say "pray" and to say "plead in a court of law". Mary Baker Eddy refers to this aspect of the prayer in her allegory which is on page 430 of *Science and Health* where a sick man defends his cause in a court.

In a court, one does not speak to himself, but rather to the judge or to the opposing party. Thus in the process of the purification when we affirm our purity in the present, the past and the future, we do not speak to ourselves, because that would be autosuggestion. But we address ourselves rather either to the Supreme Being, or to Christ, i.e., to the saints, or to the carnal mind which is the opposing party.

When we address ourselves to the Supreme Being, our prayer is a prayer of gratitude, because actually we do not ask God to render us pure, but we thank Him for having created us pure. But when we address ourselves to Christ, i.e., to the saints who support us, our prayer is also a request for justice. However the assertion of our purity while addressing ourselves to God or to Christ must also be an acceptance of our Christ nature.

104

When we address ourselves to the carnal mind, our prayer is an argumentation: an assertion of the truth and a negation of the error.

To talk to oneself in the process of purification is autosuggestion and that at long run does not any more give any good result, this bad mental practice separates us from God while making us believe that the power to heal is personal.

13.14. All is pure for those who are pure (Titus 1: 15)

The first stage when one launches out in the search of spirituality is to become aware of its own purity. But at a certain stage of spiritual development one realizes that to purify oneself is to also become aware that all are pure. Understanding this, Jesus taught his disciples to pray in the first person of plural: "Our Father which art in heavens..." We are pure because God, the All-in-all, is pure, consequently all are pure.

The expert of the divine science who understands this reality can thus affirm: "I am pure, I was always pure and I would be always so, because God is All and all is pure, sin never had the power to do us good, therefore it cannot have the power to separate us from God..."

13.15. Conclusion

The notion of the divine Word is essential to the devoutness in the high Bantu spiritual tradition. This concept is identical to the notion of Christ in Christian Science. The Christ is inseparable from man, but this complete nature of being must be accepted and lived by each one of us. Thus the prayer in Bantu divine science, consists in becoming aware of the Christ in oneself to become aware of the Christ around oneself; i.e., to become aware of the holiness in oneself so that the presence of the saint-ancestors around oneself becomes tangible. God always acts by the Christ and in the double dimension of the Christ: the holiness which abides in man and the holiness which surrounds man.

14. THE ILLUSORY NATURE OF WITCHCRAFT

More than one person walking at night took a stump of a tree for an evil appearance. The ignorance of the surrounding may force people in this case to find salvation in running. Yet to the daylight we all realize that the devil was a visual illusion. To scold and tackle what appeared to be a nocturnal threat denotes fear and attributes a "reality" to illusion.

The only real cure is to realize the nothingness of illusion, refuse to give a reality to the belief in a truly present and powerful devil. This illustrates what should be our attitude toward witchcraft. Rather than addressing an illusion (the witch and his fetishes), we must block access to our thought to any the belief in a power, a presence and a reality of witchcraft.

I reached a point in my academic studies where everything seemed to stagnate. I had the clear conviction that a witch was manipulating me and undermining any success. Yielding to this belief, I endeavored, through prayer, to destroy the fetishes and the alleged "powers" of this witch-cousin, but that led only to a worse situation.

At this point I sincerely and humbly turned to God to be enlightened. I then realized that by tackling an illusion, I had made a reality of it. I had succumbed to the belief that it is my cousin who had to change. Whenever in reality, I had to change my way of seeing the situation from the perfection of man (my cousin and me) as the image and likeness of God.

Divine Science teaches us that God is Mind, the only true source of our ideas. It is the divine Mind that acts in every man "to will and to do of [God's] good pleasure"[54]. So I realized that as an image and likeness of God, my cousin could only do that which is good.

I realized that I did not have to hate my cousin, or to believe that he hates me. Because to believe that someone hates you, is to entertain the belief in hatred and expose oneself to its venom. This understanding allowed me to heal what appeared to be a situation beyond any effort of prayer.

Whatever its appearance, evil is only a suggestion that comes to our mind. The solution to the problem of witchcraft is not to mentally manipulate our environment, or even to manipulate our own person, but to refuse access to our own mind to any malicious suggestion.

Witchcraft has only the power that we give it and not the power it assumes. It is in being based on this understanding that we can fight against this scourge. Forgetting this reality, humanity invites failure in the fight against this evil scourge, since it is seeking solutions elsewhere than in itself.

The darkness can not exist in a consciousness filled with light. God expresses in us the illumination of the Word. The awareness of the constant presence of God in us and around us closes the door to any hint of evil and allows us to overcome all its claims.

---

[54] *Philippiens* 2: 13.

15. DEFEATING WITCHCRAFT

The belief in witchcraft is one of the great difficulties the church faces in Africa. The praiseworthy efforts carried out in order to dame up this plague have remained without notable success. Today many researchers realize that the simple stereotype in answer to the question of the existence of witchcraft in terms of a categorical yes or no is not anymore enough.[55] the victory over witchery thus rests on a balanced understanding of the claims of witchcraft and the nothingness of these claims.

For a greater efficiency in the fight against witchcraft, we must initially restore the truth concerning this malefic practice: what is witchcraft and in what is it different from the African mystery (called by the Bakongo *kindoki*[2])?

We will explore two approaches, which are the current ways of understanding the problem of the *kindoki* (wrongfully called witchcraft): the rational demonstration and the pragmatic approach. We will then expose the approach that we recommend for this problem.

The problem of witchcraft in Congo (as everywhere in Africa) is as old as the modern history of the Democratic republic of Congo. J. de Munk in its book *Kinkulu kia nsieto ya Kongo* quotes the case of King Henrique whose clan (Nimi a Vuzi) was driven out of Mbanza Kongo by Kiowa who

---

[55] Confer *Witchcraft destroying the Catholic Church in Africa, experts say*, www.catholic.org.

accused its members of witchery.[56] For the Bakongo thus witchcraft has always been a problem to be solved and they imagined for this whole panoply of solutions including the famous test of poison.

However the requirements of the academic knowledge changed the data. Because nothing can be accepted in the learned milieus that reason does not grasp. Thus one of the steps taken by a certain number of researchers is to prove the existence of witchcraft rationally. It is in this context that we can situate, for example, the approach of Prof. Buakasa who in *Discours sur la kindoki ou sorcellerie*, on the basis of the examples drawn from daily life, seeks to prove the existence of witchcraft rationally.[4] This approach has the advantage of bringing the problems of the *kindoki* in the curriculums of modern learned societies, but it doesn't advance us in the direction of the resolution of the basic problem: how to overcome witchcraft?

Concurrently to this approach is the pragmatic one, which, on the basis of the recognition that the problem is a social fact, seeks to find the solution to it. Here one can quote, for instance, Prof. Kimpianga who in his book *la Problématique crocodilienne à Luozi*, after having explored the Kongo deep thought relating to the *kindoki* and witchcraft, tries to give a solution to a formerly current practice of witchcraft in the *manianga* area (in DRC): the phenomenon of crocodiles tamed for malefic uses.[57]

---

[56] J. de Munck, *Kinkulu kia nsi eto a Kongo*, Tumba, 1971, p.46.

Though we don't reject the approach of the rational demonstration used by Prof. Buakasa, we prefer the pragmatic approach to it, but not without bringing a complementary of light. Because the difficulty that these two approaches present is that they don't care about the existence of two ways of thinking in the world: the rational thinking, based on the reason, and a second way of thinking anchored in the soul thus we will call it the *amimic* thinking. Didn't Senghor say: "reason is Hellenic, while emotion is Black?"

In our book titled: *Vaincre la sorcellerie en Afrique*[58], we showed that the West and Africa present two different forms of thinking, fruits of centuries-old heritages, one is based on the reason, while the other is anchored in the soul. These two ways of thinking are curiously reflected by the natures of these two milieus.

The West is the milieu of the man who is the direct heir to the tribes which fled the icy climate of the polar regions of the North. The climatic context of the West is characteristically cold, whereby all tends to crystallize, to take a definite form. It is thus the world of the visible, the tangible, and the palpable where intellect plays a paramount role.

The African, on the other hand, lives in a torrid climate and is heir to the tribes which lived the areas then torrid of the South and the East of the Mediterranean. In this climatic

---

[57] Kimpianga Mahaniah, *la Problèmatique crocodilienne à Luaozi*, Kinshasa, 1989.

[58] Kiatezua L. Luyaluka, *Vaincre la sorcellerie en Afrique*, Harmattan, 2009.

context, constantly "burned" by the sun, things tend to expand, to evaporate. It is the universe of the invisible, the intangible, the impalpable, of the *animic*, where the soul plays a central role.

The rational thinking perceives the phenomena in a physical approach via reason. All that eludes reason is rejected and qualified as superstitious. It accepts revelation only insofar as this one is verified by reason.

For the *animic* thinking the phenomena are inseparable from the mental, the physical universe is only the consequence of the activity of the ethereal plans. The *animic* thinking, the field of intuition and illumination, where the *kindoki* (properly called in French mystery) plays a central role, accepts reason only insofar as it yields to the supremacy of revelation.

The rational and the *animic* thinking are two human ways of thinking which exclude each other on the human level; each one accepting the other only insofar as it yields to its supremacy.

Consequently, to require of the scientific rational thinking to accept the existence of witchcraft, an *animic* phenomenon, is to require of it to recognize its limits and to accept the *animic* thinking and thus to start yielding ground to it. This difficulty summarizes the limit of the rational demonstration approach.

Pragmatism thus invites the African to observe the phenomenon of witchcraft as an *animic* fact and to bring in solutions on the basis of *animic* considerations.

Considered under the angle of *animic* thinking, the *kindoki* and witchcraft present two different natures:

- The *kindoki* is a knowledge and a power while witchcraft is the malefic use of a knowledge and/or a power

- The *kindoki* in the time of our ancestors was a factor of development, because, it is among the *bandoki* (those who have the knowledge of *kindoki*) that was sought, for example, the elite of the Kongo nation. Speaking of the Lemba initiatory academy, Fukiau wrote in *le Mukongo et le monde qui l'entourait:* "All those who had attended Lemba became important men, very known; they became leaders: governors, judges, healers; etc." [59] But witchcraft is always a factor of underdevelopment because, it destroys social fabric.

- The objective of witchcraft is primarily to destroy, dominate or steal; while the *kindoki* was initially a knowledge related to the religious practice, a tool for maintaining order, for protection and progress of society. The *bandoki* (plural of *ndoki*) formed the elite of the Kongo society.

- The *kindoki* had official settings of teaching (initiatory schools), while sorcery was always a deviation condemned by society.

The difference between *kindoki* and witchcraft can be elucidated by replacing the term *kindoki* in its true etymological context. Witchcraft is defined as the use of malefic spirits for

---

[59] A. Fukiau, *le Mukôngo et le monde qui l'entourait*, Kinshasa, p.133.

the purpose of harming, while the words *kindoki* and *ndoki* deals with the product of the African pre-colonial educational system.

Contrary to the general belief, the word *ndoki* does not derive from the word *loka* - which, by the way, should not be translated by "cursing" (*sînga* in *kikôngo*) but rather by "warning in prayer".

We show in: *Vaincre la sorcellerie en Afrique* that the word *ndoki* comes from the word *doka* which, as the meanings of the words of the same family indicate, refers to the educational system of our ancestors, whose three stages were symbolized by: death, resurrection, life among the spirits, and rebirth. In *kikôngo* one forms the word which designates the person performing the action of the word by adding n' before the infinitive and by substituting the termination a by i, except for the monosyllabic verbs and those starting with f, v, w, p, and b.

Example:

- *luka* = vomit; *n'luki* = the one who vomit.

- *Losa* = throw; *n'losi* = the thrower.

- *Sika* = fire; *n'siki* = the one who fires.

- *Yemba* = steal; *n'yembi* = the stealer.

According to this rule, from the word *loka* comes the word *n'loki*, and the word *ndoki* must come from the word *doka*. Thus one can still find the true meaning of the word *ndoki* by

115

referring to the words of the same family and by examining the pre-colonial educational system. Education in pre-colonial Africa, as in the Egypt of the Pharaohs, comprised 3 phases symbolizing: death, life among the "spirits", and rebirth.

The first phase consisted in subjecting negative emotions and human will. Now one finds in the family of *ndoki* words related to submission:

- *Dokisa* = to subject,

- *Dokama* = to bend oneself,

- *Doka* = to stoop down, from where one draws *n'doki* = the one who is subjected.

In this phase the initiate was sometimes subjected to painful tests, like circumcision. One was then exhorted to show courage, endurance and heroism. One finds in the family of *ndoki* the following words related to exhortation:

- *Dodikila* = to exhort.

- *Dokalala* = exhorted.

- *Doka* = persuaded.

In the second phase, symbolizing life among the spirits, the initiate learned the secret teachings; it is the phase of instruction expressed by the following words:

- *Kindokila* = slapping of two fingers to ask to speak; the one who raises questions. A Kongo proverb says:

"*Kindokila mumbuesa diela.*" (He who raises questions increases the intelligence of several people.)

- *Dokidika* = to instruct. From which one draws: *kidokidika* = to learn; and *kidokidiki*, a synonym of *ndoki* in the meaning "the one who learns."

One finds several pairs of this kind in *kikôngo*. Example:

- o To block = *kaka; kakidika*.

- o To deposit = *lumba; lumbidika*.

From which one draws:

- o *N'kaki* = *kikakidiki* = the one who blocks;

- o *Nlumbi* = *kilumbidiki* = the one who deposits;

- o *Ndoki* = *kidokidiki* = the one who learns;

- *Doka* = to inculcate; whereby one draws *n'doki* = the teacher.

"In the forth phase, symbolizing rebirth, the initiate having given up a vile personality was now born again; his knowledge was extended and his ethereal faculties awaked or extended. The following words of the family of *ndoki* evoke this phase:

- *Doka* = to extend.

- *Makutu ma doka* = sharp ears (hearing).

All this development shows that the *kindoki* is only knowledge which allows one to improve his spiritual and intellectual faculties. The ultimate goal of education has always been the perception of what is invisible to the uneducated. For the *animic* thinking, this perception of the invisible is called the *kindoki* and can be acquired apparently in three ways:

- Through the purification of the thought, divine method[s].[60]

- Through human means.

- Through the means of the malefic spirits, demonic method.

Due to the confusion maintained between the African mystery and witchcraft, in the majority of African languages there are two words to designate witchcraft. Actually one of these two words means mystery and it has an ambivalent nature; because the African, deep in his heart, feels that this word refers to a positive concept. And the other word is a completely negative one and it means witchcraft.

Example:

- Among the Bakongo of Congo: *kindoki* (mystery) and *n'soki* (witchcraft).

---

[60] Voir *Matthieu* 5:8.

- Among the Luba-Kasai of the Democratic republic of Congo: *bumpongo* (mystery) and *buloji* (witchcraft).

- For the Douala of Cameroun: *lemba* (mystery) and *ewusu* (witchcraft).

- For the Bomitaba of the Republic of Congo: *buanga* (mystery) and *bolemba* (witchcraft).

- For the Babindja of DRC: Mabôka (mystery) and buanga (witchcraft).

- Etc.

The *kindoki* acquired by the divine means can be used only positively. In the second case the *kindoki* can be used positively or negatively. In the demonic method the *kindoki* can be used only negatively i.e. in witchcraft.

It is here that the pragmatism of the Institut des Sciences Animiques (ISA) which we direct offers a singular solution to the problem of the *kindoki* and witchcraft, solution inspired from the Afrocentric spiritual tradition. The ISA shows that the problem of witchcraft and that of the *kindoki* must be approached in two different ways.

About the *kindoki* we must know that in any *animic* society the majority is recruited in the camp of the *kindoki* acquired by human means. Thus, the progress or the decline of African societies depends on the nature of the influence which this majority undergoes. The influence of the divine *kindoki* brings development, while the influence of the demonic *kindoki* leads to decline. Thus we must work to fight the demonic *kindoki*, insofar as it can lead only to witchcraft, therefore to decline; as for the human *kindoki*, we must work for its elevation, i.e., we must work so as those who possess it may use it only for good purposes. And the manner of obliging them to use this potential only in good ways is the prayer of warning that we show lower in the book.

To fight witchcraft, we must know that its alleged power is intrinsic and extrinsic:

- Extrinsic: the victim lends power to witchcraft by his fear and his hatred of the witch and his ignorance of witchcraft.

- Intrinsic: the witch believes that he is animated by spirits and believes he acts as a spirit.

We must also know that witchcraft always acts through suggestion. But these suggestions can be made in three ways: through thinking, through words, or through acts. In all the three cases, the important thing is to know how to close the door to these suggestions; because it is the victim himself who gives the power to these suggestions.

Thus the work against witchcraft includes primarily five steps:

- Purification of oneself.

- Negation of the belief in spiritualism.

- Negation of the possibilities of the malefic suggestions.

- Negation of witchcraft.

- Warning.

Purification: we can fight more efficiently witchcraft only insofar as we are based on the divine mystery, on the power that the divine Word confers to man; hence the need of purification. Because this one is a precondition for the one who, like on the mountain of transfiguration, wants to attract to himself the succor of the celestial army of the saints, the army "the spirits of just men made perfect"[61]. To purify ourselves is to understand that sin actually has never done us good, that it can never do us good. Thus on this basis we must separate ourselves from sin and determine to walk in purity.

Negation of spiritualism: the devil claims to be a spirit, but we also know that he is a liar, and that there is no truth in him.[62] Hence we must realize (or affirm) that God is the only true Spirit which controls us and controls actually the so-called witch. Such a conviction strips witchcraft of all alleged power, because if God is the Spirit which acts in the so-called witch, then this one can only do what is good.[63]

---

[61] Voir *Epitre aux Hébreux* 12: 23.

[62] *Jean* 8: 44.

[63] Voir *Philippiens* 2: 13.

Negation of the possibilities of the malefic suggestions: we must realize (or affirm) that God is the only true source of our thoughts and the thoughts of the so-called witch, consequently there is no other mind from which malefic suggestions can proceed against us or against anyone. The importance of this affirmation is that witchcraft always acts through suggestions, as underlined above. Thus as long as we do not accept the suggestions, witchcraft does not have an influence on us, but since the acceptance of the suggestions can be done in the unconsciousness, it is thus important to deny the possibility of the malefic suggestions consciously.

Negation of sorcery: on the basis of what precedes we must affirm the nothingness of witchcraft by understanding that it has neither power, neither reality, nor presence because God is All-in-all, thus all in the universe of God, expresses His power and His presence.

Warning: we make the warning through God. For that we ask Him: "Lord, opens the eyes of the so-called witch that he may know that the evil he does to others returns violently towards himself and that witchcraft leads him even now to death." Contrary to the current practice of the New-born Churches, the warning is not a request made to God to destroy the sinners, who actually are also children of God, but unaware of their true condition. The warning is based on love and aims at forcing the witch to choose between life (by shunning evil) and death.

The victory against witchcraft is a precondition for the true development of Africa; but to fight this plague efficiently, it is necessary for us first of all to distinguish it from the *kindoki* (the African mystery), because the confusion of these two concepts is a great factor of failure. A rationalistic attitude which limits itself to the denial of the existence of witchcraft cannot help Africa in its fight against the claims of witchcraft. Witchcraft can and must be overcome by an approach which strips it of its alleged power and forces the witch to choose between reforms and the boomerang effect which leads to death.

16. BANISH FEAR

"Know, O my brother, fear is a great obstacle."[64] This was taught by Thoth, the Atlantean, addressing the people of

Khem (ancient Egypt). Fear is the biggest obstacle on the path of the enlightenment of humanity, on the way the spiritual progress and the liberation of the soul from the shackles of bodily senses. Almost all the problems faced by humanity can be reduced to a fear maintained and which is not curbed. Thus the first step in African initiatory schools was to banish fear.

The belief in fear is based on the assumption that evil is stronger than good. This assumption leads to a conviction of insecurity. Yet Divine Science shows us that God is omnipotent. Darkness (the symbol of evil) has no power over light. And the Bible tells us that God is light and in Him there is no darkness. (I John I: 5).So evil has in reality only the power that our own belief confers it. This fear is the denial of the omnipotence of God. We must banish fear thanks to the enlightened understanding of the omnipotence of God, Love.

The Bible tells us in I John 4: 18 that: "There is no fear in love, but perfect love casts out fear; because fear involves punishment, and he who fears is not made perfect in love." Fear is therefore the belief that man can be separated from the infinite goodness of God. God is Love; He is the infinite and omnipresent source of all goodness. In the Kongo initiation divine Love is designated by the attribute Kalunga (the All-in-all), because for the Besikôngo God fills all space and everything in the universe is His manifestation, the manifestation His infinite goodness. There is therefore nothing in God's creation that can affect the safety of man, God's image; evil is an illusion that must be fought and

---

[64] *Les Chemins d'Hermès*, www.lescheminsdhermes.org.

destroyed by the conviction of the totality of God, good. Evil is not therefore part of God's creation.

The creator God in His manifestation of the infinite love of the Most High created man in His image and likeness. This likeness of man to God implies a permanent and unchanging presence of God's goodness in man and around man: the Word.[65] Man in the Divine Science is inseparable from the Word. God never removes the Word from man whatever be the acts of the latter. So the Word is eternally in man for his salvation. The Word eternally expresses in man and around man all the infinite goodness of God, without violating the free will that God has given to His children.

It is imperative for humanity to understand that fear is not always just a feeling of insecurity that makes the heart pounds. Fear is sometimes a subtle feeling that we accept without even realizing it. From the perspective of its subtlety, fear is one of the characteristics of the lunar thinking in which humanity evolves now; or to put it better, a thinking in which the Black-man evolves blindly today and where he slavishly apes the Westerner in science, politics and religion…

As the moon is a planet that revolves around the earth, the lunar thinking is a mainly limited thinking, a thinking whose basic presuppositions are limitations; because the lunar thinking begins with the material limited vision and/or reverse

---

[65] The notion of the Word corresponds to the notion of Horus in the Osirian initiation, to the notion of the Kimahungu in the Kongo initiation et to the notion of Christ in the Christian initiation.

reality. The very characteristic of lunar thinking, the materialistic rationalism of the West, is that it starts from imperfection to perfection. Man in the rationalistic conception is an imperfect mortal who must. at all costs, to avoid perishing, improve, add the property to his imperfect existence and he often feels compelled to do so at the expense of others. Western rationalistic thought starting with the belief in limitation, is essentially a subtle suggestion of fear. Mankind is led to fear when it accepts that:

- Tomorrow fossil fuels will run out, hence the need to accumulate reserves of oil and to spoil other people (the weak) of their reserves by unfair exploitation, abuse and imperialism.

- The offer in the job market is limited, hence we must have the best training possible.

- Customers are limited and competition is inevitable and all means are good to ward off potential opponents.

- Etc.

I do not sustain that fossil fuels will continue infinitely, I'm not saying that it is not necessary to have the best possible training, but I would argue that any action of humanity that share the belief that the goods are essentially limited, builds on fear. Understanding this Thoth, the Atlantean, already advised at his time the Africans (of yesterday like those of today) not to be seduced by the materialistic rationalism of the West: "Do not let yourself be seduced by brothers of darkness who show you the OBSCURE LIGHT. The reflected light is not the sunlight. Do not let yourself be seduced by the artificial light they want to project to you to give you the illusion that you exist. You're the center; you're the one who enlightens. You're SUN LIGHT of your universe. Always keep your eyes in this direction and your soul in accordance with THE CENTRAL LIGHT."[66]

To live without fear is to live first of all by basing one's action on the presupposition of the solar thinking that good is unlimited, because good is God. Just as the earth revolves around the sun, solar thinking is the one in which humanity naturally turns toward the Creator: the Sun of suns. Unlike lunar thinking, solar thinking, the enlightened thinking which is the quintessence of the true Black soul, starts from perfection (God) to the nothingness of imperfection (evil): man is the image and likeness of God; it is on this basis that he must demonstrate his perfection, the perfection of his neighbor and the nothingness of evil. Solar thinking is a thinking that is based on love. That is why Afrocentric wisdom insists: "*Tonda nkuêno bu utôndanga nitu aku.*"[67] (Love your neighbor as you love your own body.)

In accordance therefore with the solar thinking, our nations must build reserves of oil, not because it will be running out tomorrow, but for the sake of conformity to the divine wisdom which should characterize our management. Young people must provide themselves the best possible training, not

---

[66] Ibidem.

[67] Precept of the Kimpasi, one of the Kongo initiatory academies.

due to fear of competition on the job market, but because they need to manifest the infinite intelligence that God, Mind, expresses in them. The trader should seek the customer, not due to fear of limitation, but based on the belief that they are infinite and available at all, etc. Such an approach to the action of man opens the door to opportunities unexpected that fear seeks to hide and this approach avoids conflicts between men and nations.

One day someone came to see me for an employment related problem. He was a candidate for a position in a cabinet, but the problem was that there was, as always in such cases, many candidates for so few jobs. I made him understand that this is an erroneous view that made him believe that there was a limited supply. I made him understand that God has jobs for everyone and that some of the candidates (maybe himself too) had their opportunity elsewhere and that our prayer must be based on the conviction of the abundance of God's goodness to assist and help others to find their place in the job market. When the list of people selected to work in this ministerial cabinet came out, he was not discouraged to see that his name was not included; he was convinced that no limit is part of the divine economy. Several months later, he was called and was able to work in this office until the end of the term of the Minister. To banish fear is first of all to think and act from the base of the perfection of man as the image of God, on the basis of God's omnipresence and omnipotence and on the basis of the abundance of good.

To banish fear is to turn away from the lunar thinking and its subtle fears and base one's thinking and actions on the solar thinking, the thinking that is called to govern the world in the third millennium. Humanity must thus place great hope today in the revival of *animicist* mentality[68], because the Bible predicts that the moon will be under the feet of the woman and the stars (the suns) will crown her head. (Apocalypse 12: 1)

17. THE EPISTLE TO THE HEBREWS

The *Epistle to the Hebrews* is one of the biblical texts which show us the Hebrews' way of praying. It is the initiatory book par excellence of the Hebrews. This book is also very close to

---

[68] Thought based on the freedom soul and in which intuition has supremacy above reason.

our African traditions and can thus guide us to reconcile our traditional spirituality and Christianity. In

All over Africa, the Black, in his higher religiosity, prayed God through the intercession of his ancestors. It belongs to us to see how to reconcile this way of praying of our ancestors with Christianity, otherwise, modern religions will remain only a frontage which hides African customs that one seeks perhaps to destroy by ignorance or by ill will.

The African always had a high spiritual tradition that should not be rejected, but integrated in the religious practice by making its second reading through divine Science. This second reading of our spiritual traditions allows us, to decode the African rites, to seize its deep sense and to give up material rites for a more spiritual approach.

The author of the *Epistles to the Hebrews* recommended the same step to his people; he asked them to give up a ritual and materialistic approach of the worship for a completely spiritual approach, based on the Word (Christ), the divine nature in man and around man.

The goal of true religion among Hebrews, as among Africans, was to lead man to be able to listen to oracles of God and to a higher degree, to lead him to be able to see the saints face to face. *The Epistle to the Hebrews* shows the believers how to achieve this broad goal of religion. *The Epistle to the Hebrews* shows us the nature and the importance of the prayer of the intercession of the saint-ancestors. It is important for the African of to today to work to find two elements which he lost in the contact with the West: the aptitude to fight efficiently witchcraft and the connection with the saint-ancestors. On the mastery of these two elements depends the true progress on the black continent; *The Epistle to the Hebrews* opens the way towards this discovery.

Heb. 1: 1 – 2: Long ago, at many times and in many ways, God spoke to our fathers by the prophets, but in these last days he has spoken to us by his Son, whom he appointed the heir of all things, through whom also he created the world.

Humanity always believed that revelation is a particular gift that only a limited number of elected people can have; these elected are called here the prophets. But, in reality, God gives revelation to all those who prepare themselves to receive them. He who becomes aware of the presence of the Word in him can receive from God revelations; Mary Baker Eddy wrote in *Unity of the Good*: "He is near to them who adore Him."[69] (To adore means also to contemplate with admiration and respect.) God speaks to all humanity, but only those who become aware of the Word in them and around them perceives His voice. To be able to receive oracles from God is the destination of the disciple among Africans and Hebrews.

Heb. 1: 3: He is the radiance of the glory of God and the exact imprint of his nature, and he upholds the universe by the word of his power. After making purification for sins, he sat down at the right hand of the Majesty on high,

If Jesus did not enter the Holy of Holies, the most high place, without purifying himself first, how then Christians can claim to enter therein without purification? Mary Baker Eddy

---

[69] Mary Baker Eddy, *Unité du Bien*, (Boston: CSPS), p. 4:1

says in *Science and Health with the Key to the Scriptures*: "We should strive to reach the Horeb height where God is revealed; and the corner-stone of all spiritual building is purity. The baptism of Spirit, washing the body the impurities of flesh, signifies that the pure in heart see God and are approaching spiritual Life and its demonstration."[70]

The Bible says of Jesus (I Pierre 2: 22): "He committed no sin, neither was deceit found in his mouth." Of which sin then did he purify himself? The reformer Eddy says: "Jesus experienced few of the pleasures of the physical senses, but his sufferings were the fruits of other people's sins, not of his own."[71] If Jesus experienced even a few beliefs in the pleasures in the matter, how is he still without sin?

In her interpretation of the Lord's prayer Mary Baker Eddy says: "For God is infinite, all-power (...)"[72] Notice here that she uses IS and not HAS. As God is all-power, can evil have any power? Does sin have a power when God is all-power? Does sin have the ability to hide in your past as to become something irremediable? Does sin have the ability to become an integral part of your existence? Actually God being all-power, sin does not have the ability to become a reality in our past, thus sin is always a present temptation, a lie, an illusion in

---

[70] Mary Baker Eddy, *Science et Santé avec la Clé des Ecritures*, (Boston: CSPS), p. 241

[71] Ibidem p. 38

[72] Ibidem, p. 17

the present. Jesus knew it and he did not grant reality to this present illusion, hence he was without sin.

You will certainly say to me: but if somebody stole a goat five years ago, this sin is certainly in his past. I will retort you not; the only sin of which he has to get rid of is the present belief that this sin made him good, that he benefitted from it and that this sin has the ability to separate somebody from a good and to give it to another. If he can get rid of this present belief now, then he is without sin. We will be without sin when we will understand this great truth: that sin is not an irremediable fact in our past, but it is always an untrue belief in the present. The only sin we have to get rid of is the present belief that sin made us good, or makes us good, or that it will be able to make us good, but also the belief that sin can deprive our next of a good or has deprived our next of a good. If we get rid of this present belief, we are like Jesus without sin.

Heb. 2: 17: Therefore he had to be made like his brothers in every respect, so that he might become a merciful and faithful high priest in the service of God, to make propitiation for the sins of the people.

Our mission, as that of Jesus, is both individual and collective; so we do the purification not only for us, but also for the people. And in the practice of spiritual therapeutic, we make the purification not only for us but also for our patient. This represents the double nature of the Word (Christ), because God is in us and around us.

Heb. 3: 19: So we see that they were unable to enter because of unbelief.

They could not enter not because of their sin, but because of their incredulity, their refusal to accept that the Word is the only true present nature of man; because of their refusal to accept that they had only to get rid of their present belief that sin made them good, or that it makes them good. Did they only get rid of this belief they would have been without sin like Jesus and free to enter the holiest place.

What prevents us from entering the holiest place is not the power of sin (since there is none, because God is all-power) but our refusal to separate ourselves from the belief that sin made us good, or that it can do us good and this present belief is the only sin which one must get rid of.

Heb. 4: 1: Let us therefore fear, lest, a promise being left us of entering into his rest, any of you should seem to come short of it.

Mary Baker Eddy says: "Beloved brethren, Christ, Truth, saith unto you, "Be not afraid!" — fear not sin, lest thereby it master you; but only fear to sin."[73] *To fear sin* is to believe that sin has a power (that implies also the belief that it can do good). He who fears sin cannot exert dominion over sin. *To fear to sin* is to beware to not fall into the temptation to believe that sin made us good or that it has the power to do us good. To fear to sin is to beware to exert one's dominion over sin. The acrobat who walks on the rope does not fear the fall, but he fears to fall, i.e., he takes care not to fall; while the one who cannot walk of a rope fears the fall, he believes that he will fall if he dared. We are called to serve God by unveiling the

---

[73] May Baker Eddy, *Ecrits Divers*, (Boston: CSPS), p 109

nothingness of sin for ourselves and for the people; for ourselves and for Africa. But to unveil the nothingness of sin does not simply consist in saying: "sin does not exist." We must understand that there is no pleasure in sin.

Heb. 6: 11-12: And we desire that every one of you do shew the same diligence to the full assurance of hope unto the end: That ye be not slothful, but followers of them who through faith and patience inherit the promises.

The Jews tried to reach perfection through the sacrifice of blood of bulls. But this rite was only a transitory stage towards the true sacrifice which brings true sanctification: the sacrifice of the belief of the pleasure in sin, through the authority of the Word.

Heb. 7: 25: Wherefore [Jesus] is able also to save them to the uttermost that come unto God by him, seeing he ever liveth to make intercession for them.

To approach God by Jesus, it is to approach God by the Christ, the Word; by becoming aware of the double dimension of the Word, i.e., by becoming aware of the presence of God in us (the inner dimension of the Word) through the purification of thought and by becoming aware of the presence of God around us (the outer dimension of the Word), in other words, by becoming aware of divine holiness around us.

Heb. 10: 22: Let us draw near with a true heart in full assurance of faith, having our hearts sprinkled from an evil conscience, and our bodies washed with pure water.

Here the author reminds to us once again that the way leading to the Holy of Holies is the purification of one's thought.

Heb. 12: 18: For ye are not come unto the mount that might be touched, and that burned with fire, nor unto blackness, and darkness, and tempest,

The goal of prayer is not a material elevation of the thought. Our goal in prayer is to reach the conscience of the Truth, the conscience of the allness of God and the nothingness of matter (the belief in the limitation of good and in evil), because it is this Christ-conscience that brings healing.

When Jesus "yielded up the ghost" the veil of the temple hiding the Holy of Holies was torn, symbolizing that the separation between the people and the Holy of holies never existed. The Jews believed in the existence of this separation, hence only the high priest entered the Holy of holies, while the African divine spirituality teaches that man walks day by day along with the Holy of holies and can reach to it thanks to the double dimension of the Word.

The Holy of Holies has never been behind a veil, but it was always on the spiritual heights that each one of us can and must endeavor to reach through to the spiritualization of the consciousness and the negation of the belief in witchcraft. When we scan the African traditions in the light of this great revelation of *the Epistle to the Hebrews,* we can then say that the saint-ancestors are not in a cemetery where we must go to seek them, but that they are in water, i.e., in a world of holiness (because water is the symbol of holiness in Africa).

Heb. 12: 22-23: But ye are come unto mount Sion, and unto the city of the living God, the heavenly Jerusalem, and to an innumerable company of angels, To the general assembly and church of the firstborn, which are written in heaven, and to God the Judge of all, and to the spirits of just men made perfect,

Here the author shows us what the Holy of holies is really. The "just men made perfect", as we all must know are nothing other than saint-ancestors. They thus are part of the celestial army and are ready to help us if we open our thought to their presence. The Word is not only the divine ego of man, but also the holiness which surrounds his being and which is symbolized by the presence of saint-ancestors around him.

Heb. 12: 25: See that ye refuse not him that speaketh. For if they escaped not who refused him that spake on earth, much more shall not we escape, if we turn away from him that speaketh from heaven:

Here the author of the Epistle to the Hebrews shows us the goal of our spiritual trip, a mental trip achieved by the purification of thought. The goal of this spiritual elevation is thus to be able to hear to oracles of God. God speaks to all of us and at any moment; and through purification and through the prayer of the intercession of saint-ancestors each one of us hastens this happy day where he will be able to hear the voice of God through saint-ancestors and even see them. To be face to face with saint-ancestors is thus the great goal of religion among Africans as well as among the Hebrews. This way of praying thus helps us not only to find the way of the high spirituality of our ancestors, but also the way of the true spirituality taught and lived by Jesus.

18. THE REAL SUBSTANCE OF BEING

For a long time I often asked myself the question: what is the translation of the word "matter" in the language of my ethnic group, the Kikongo? I tried several concepts to translate the idea of matter in Kikongo, until I came to the conclusion that my Black African ancestors had no conception of the substance as being physical!

The African has always conceived that the real substance of being is the Spirit and that what appears to be a physical appearance is only a limitation, an illusion. The Bassa of Cameroon remind us of this reality of the Afrocentric divine spirituality when they call the man they see "*mut Binam.*" This means: "the man who has two legs and two hands?" The Bassa imply by this that the real man (*mut*) is the reality that the corporeal senses can not grasp and which is weakly expressed by the visible man.

Such a view of things may seem shocking to our rationalistic education. Indeed, rationalistic sciences tell us that the universe is composed of a substance called "matter." It should be emphasized that, contrary to what the common man thinks, these modern sciences have not demonstrated the actual existence of a material substance. So it is by assumption that they accept this view of things!

In my book titled *la Religion Kongo*[74], I demonstrate with scientific logic thanks to a cosmological argument based on

---

[74] Kiatezua L. Luyaluka, *la Religion* Kongo, Harmattan, 2010, pp. 67-95.

the existence of individualities that what seems to be a physical reality is only a limited and/or reverse perception the reality of being, which reality is totally spiritual. This Afrocentric scientific concept of substance, strange to Western rationalistic thinking, is rather always present in our everyday experience.

Imagine yourself as being in a sunny day, the sky is clear and you see a plane (of a DC 10 type) fly a few miles above your head. If I ask you: how it appears? You may say that it is very small according to your personal material senses. But if I ask you: how the airplane is actually (a DC-10)? You will say: very large; referring to the characteristics of this plane carrying 250 passengers, 10 tons of fuel and 40 tons of cargo. But, without doubt, in your belief, there are not two planes: one small and the other great. The small plane that you seem to see is the great; so you use more than your physical senses to identify the reality of the aircraft, you use your understanding of aeronautics.

Along with this analogy of the aircraft, Divine Science asks us to go beyond the appearances to understand that man and the universe are even now spiritual, where they seem to be material. *The Epistle to the Hebrews* affirms this state of affairs when we learn that: "Through faith we understand that the worlds were framed by the word of God, so that things which are seen were not made of things which do appear."[75]

Even where he seems to be limited and vitiated by errors (sin, disease and death), man is actually composed of all the

---

[75] Epistle to the Hebrew 11: 3.

infinite qualities of Spirit. Even where there seems to be a physical heart, man has an infinite generosity which is the only reality of his heart; even where there seems to be a pair of limited eyes, man has an infinite perception which actually constitutes his eyes; even where there seems to be two arms, man manifests unlimited activity, the reality of his arms. However, we do not care to know absolutely what quality is really every organ of our being; we just need to understand that where there seems to be limited organs, man actually has infinite spiritual qualities.

Contemplating the material order of things Thoth of Atlantis, the initiator of all the wisdom of Egypt (the same one that Moses, the Hebrew prophet learned and taught the Israelites - Acts 7: 22) warns us: "Remember, O man, all that exists is simply another form of what does not exist."[76] Matter, as I said above, is therefore only a limited and/or reverse perspective of the spiritual reality, the only reality that is in us and surrounds us.

This vision, so important to the divine metaphysical therapy, protects us against the belief in witchcraft. As witchcraft claims to be able to destroy and steal everything that is material or that we believe to be material. To understand that everything in us and around us is actually made of infinite spiritual qualities is an important protection against the belief that devastates all Africa.

---

[76] *Les Chemins d'Hermès*, www.lechemind'hermes.org.

After buying my first car, I stumbled with a serious difficulty; this automobile fell down all the time. I was so overwhelmed by the expenses occasioned that the thought of selling it haunted my spirit. Some people told me that this was normal because I bought it second hand. But I saw the situation another way and rather than give in to discouragement, I committed myself to the understanding that the car is not actually made of sheets, pillows, mechanical parts, etc.; because I knew that such enumeration also includes necessarily failures, accidents, police harassment, etc., as an integral part.

So I realized that the real car, the only that God has given me, is composed of infinite qualities such as comfort, strength, harmony, endurance, quickness, etc. The author of *Science and Health with Key Scriptures* tells us that: "All is infinite Mind and its infinite manifestation."[77] Realizing that the "all" that is referred to also includes my car, I stated that it is a manifestation of the divine Mind, a spiritual idea.

With this belief in the spiritual nature of the reality of my car, I rejected the suggestion that it could be controlled by the alleged evil forces; since I realized that God is the only Principle that governs His ideas in the comfort, strength, harmony, endurance, quickness, etc. In doing so I rebutted the mistaken belief that the reality of my car was completely hardware. Thanks to this understanding the constant

---

[77] Mary Baker Eddy, *Science et Santé avec la clé des Ecritures*, Boston, 1917, p. 468.

breakdowns have ceased and this car continues to help me up today.

To understand that the reality of being is spiritual makes us the master of the belief in matter and allows us to not submit to its limitations. The Scriptures and the Afrocentric spirituality tell us that God created man in His image and likeness and gave him dominion over all the earth. We can start today to exercise this domination through this spiritually positive vision of the actual substance of being: Spirit.

CONTENT

WHAT IS THE INSTITUT DES SCIENCES ANIMIQUES

The Institut des Sciences Animiques (ISA) is a center of reserch in afrocentric spirituatlity and philosophy created by Dr Kiatezua L. Luyaluka (Ph.D. Honours in Theology). The Iainms at the understanding of:

- The true and the highest adrocentric spirituality, its Egyptian origins and its convergence with Christianity.

- The necessity and the pertinence of the afrocentric epistemology for the scientific, technologιcal, cultural and political progress of the Black man.

- The efficiency of the fight against witchcraft.

Dr Kiatezua shares his experience of divine metaphysics accumulated since 34 years by organizing seminars on spirituality and the fight against witchcraft. To learn more about ISA go to our blog:

www.animic.wordpress.com

To contact us :

E-mail: isa.ongd@yahoo.fr
Tél. : 00243999935562
00242053214614

TO BE READ: KEMETIC THOUGHT

Quarterly journal of afrocentric spirituality, Kemetic Though presents Black-African religion by exposing its high theology and its practical import. This journal of ISA shows also to the Black-African man the necessity of an epistemological revolution which must bring the supremacy of the solar thinking over the lunar thinking of the West.

From the same author

- *Vaincre la sorcellerie en Afrique*, Paris, l'Harmattan, 154 pages. This book deepens under an anthropological perspective the problematic of the fight against witchcraft.

- *La Religion kôngo, Paris, l'Harmattan, 158 pages.* This book exposes the kôngo theology, its Egyptian origins and its convergence with Christian and Egyptian religion.

- **L'Inefficacité de l'Eglise face à la sorcellerie africaine, Paris, l'Harmattan, 196 pages.** This book on theology deepens the problematic dealt with in this booklet.

From the Institut des Sciences Animiques

Books by Dr Kiatezua, on Black-African spirituality and epistemology, published by the IAS:

1. *Epistemological Bees of the Black-African lore* the Black-African thought rests on more scientific bases than the Weston thought, hence its necessity.

2. *Witchcraft and Development in Black-African Milieu,* a demonstration of the necessity and the possibility of an efficient fight against witchcraft as a preliminary to the true development of Africa. .

3. *The Enigma of the Resurrection of Jesus,* this book set the resurrection of Jesus back to its true context which far from the scholastic theological view.

4. *The Myth of Nzala Mpanda,* an hypothesis of the imminent advent of the solar thought, a way of thinking dear to the Black, according to the myth of Nzala Mpanda.

5. *Kindoki — an African mystery elucidated* This book deepens under an anthropological perspective the problematic of the fight against witchcraft.

All these books are available on www.amazon.com.
*Realized by **Ntangu-i-Fueni**, 2012.*

Printed in Great Britain
by Amazon

63118565R00087